VOLUME 2

REAL ESTATE
EDITION

MONEY
MATTERS

World's Leading Entrepreneurs Reveal their
TOP TIPS TO SUCCESS

ADAM TORRES AND
JEFFREY MOUNT

CENTURY CITY

Century City, CA

Listen to our
PODCASTS

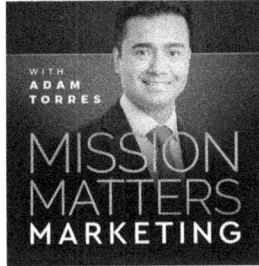

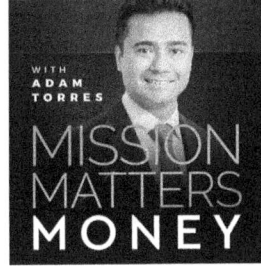

MISSION MATTERS
WE MAKE STORIES **BIGGER**

www.MissionMatters.com

For information, visit **www.MissionMatters.com**

Managing Editor:
Jyssica Schwartz

Graphic Design:
Kendra Cagle

Century City, CA 90067
www.MissionMatters.com

MISSION
MATTERS
WE MAKE STORIES BIGGER

CENTURY
CITY

The Mr. Century City Logo is a trademark of Mr. Century City, LLC.

ISBN 13: 978-1-949680-26-3

Money Matters, Beverly Hills, CA

DEDICATION

I want to dedicate this book to my family: My wife, Wendy,
my children, Phoebe, Charlie, and Skylar, and my in-laws, Jim
and Katie Stewart for their unwavering support as I transition
out of corporate America and into my entrepreneurial self.
Your confidence in me is inspirational and magical.

TABLE OF CONTENTS

ACKNOWLEDGMENTS

Bill Tweedy, President, Highline Risk Solutions

John Harrington, CFP, Integrated Financial Partners

Bob Worgaftik, President, MW Financial

David Wood, President, Gateway Financial Group

Brett Wentzell, CFP, Meritage Financial Strategies

Bill Brice and Andrea Pease, ProEast Asset Management

Kevin Ramsier and Kyle Wiggs, Exact Strategies

Joe Mallo, Financial Advisor coach

Larry Lotwin, Financial Advisor coach

Steve LePage, Financial Advisor, Cambridge Investment Research

Jody Goss and Matt Sweeney, Co-founders, William Joseph Capital
Management

Kevin Best, President, Best Times Financial

Miranda Lazzara, Financial Advisor, Progressive Investors Network LLC

Josh Wilson, President, Progressive Investors Network LLC

Eugene Harris, President, Harris Wealth Management

PREFACE

By **ADAM TORRES**

Everyone enters the real estate market for different reasons. Some do it with the hope of profits and to become professional investors while others are simply looking for a place to call home and raise a family. The first property I purchased was just to have a place to call home and it turned into a disaster. Of course, I didn't know it at the time. I was still in college and a house came on the market a couple of blocks away from my mom's house and I thought it was just great timing.

After graduation, I could move into the house and start my life. But there were a couple of things I didn't consider, being a real estate young pup and lacking life experience. First, my financing was all wrong. I was thinking I just needed to pay it off as fast as possible. So, I put the house on a 15-year mortgage. It's not like I had all of these reserves saved up, I was still in college and not able to weather any storms that may have arisen. So, I signed myself up for a high mortgage payment before I was ready for it. After all, who needs cash flow? Exactly.

Second, it was the height of the market in the early 2000s and I liked the home so much that I was willing to pay prices that the area had not seen, ever. There was a certain fervor going on in the area and in the country. Homes were selling for record prices every week. In retrospect, I heard two types of stories being told. Neophytes were buying. My friends and many other non-real-estate investor types were eager to get into the market before they "lose out on ever buying a home." The other type of story I'd hear was from real estate pros I knew and had worked for telling me how they couldn't believe how much they just sold a property for. They would tell me their original purchase price and how they had fixed the homes and held them for many years.

Does this sound familiar? "Smart money" selling into strength and "dumb money" buying.

Third, still being in college and not knowing what I wanted to do with my life, why would I have assumed I'd find employment near the neighborhood I grew up in? Or that I'd even want to live there? It was like the trifecta of inexperienced decision making at it's best.

What was the end result? I did end up paying the home off after 15 years. I rented the home to a nice family and lost $300 a month for at least 14 years of that 15-year mortgage. I didn't live in the house because I moved out of state right after college. Oh, and when I sold the home 15 years later because it basically became a waste of time and a liability, I only received about 70% of my original purchase price. The market never bounced back in the area.

Part of the reason for my bad decision making was youth and inexperience. However, that's not the real reason for my misfortune. The real reason for my misfortune was that I hadn't sought out the right mentors for the deal. To this day, I kick myself about this because they were already in my circle of influence at the time. There were people who I had access to that I could have run the deal by. But instead, I choose to ask my friends, who were less than savvy real estate investors. Imagine asking your college buddy during a party if you should buy a house. Exactly. Not the best idea.

So, why am I telling you this embarrassing story of defeat?

I could easily try to justify my defeat and say, well at least that six-figure mistake would one day save me from making a seven-figure mistake. While that is true, that's definitely selective reasoning at it's best. Can I really say that? What I did was let a $20 investment in picking up a real estate book turn into a six-figure mistake. It was just silly. Which brings me to the book you are holding in your hands.

I am excited to bring you this book in the hopes that you don't need to make some of the mistakes that I have made in the past. The idea is simple, every volume of *Money Matters Real Estate* that is released brings more ideas and knowledge to the masses. In volume one, we assembled a top group of professionals with topics ranging from best practices for hiring a contractor to mitigating the legal risks of owning commercial properties.

In this edition, *Money Matters Real Estate Volume 2*, the chapters and lessons range from real estate syndication to investing in multifamily properties. I even share my first multifamily investment experience. Let's just say, closing that one didn't go quite as smoothly as I'd hoped. But unlike the story I just shared above, that investment was quite lucrative. I'd at least learned how to run the math at that point!

And with that, I'll let you enjoy the rest of the book! Also, if you have an interesting real estate story or lesson to tell, visit us at **MissionMatters.com** to submit your pitch for one of our upcoming volumes.

Happy investing!

Adam Torrey

INTRODUCTION

By **JEFFREY MOUNT**

Investing for capital appreciation over the last ten years has been fairly easy. The American stock market has provided many opportunities to increase wealth. The low-interest-rate environment has provided inspiration for growth-oriented investors due to cheap capital for companies who want to expand. At the same time, it leaves investors with the opportunity to invest in dividend-paying stocks to meet income needs and appreciate in value, since more traditional income-generating asset classes (bonds) yield so little. Income can be generated from lots of different classes of securities: stocks, treasury bonds, municipal bonds, high-yield bonds, Master Limited Partnerships, and even options-based strategies like covered calls and put writing. However, the one asset class that historically has delivered income streams which can significantly beat other asset classes in this low-interest rate-environment is real estate. There are certainly risks to this asset class, like any other investment, and there are different challenges which need to be faced when tackling this asset class. However, the one thing that never changes is understanding how all of this fits together.

Each of us has a unique set of goals as we move through life. Many of us have our eye on retirement. Others are still thinking about how they will put their children through college. Some people take investing to a whole different level and make it their career. Others are focused on creating a legacy with their wealth. Whatever your unique circumstances are, I suggest you create a financial plan which really analyzes the consequences of each decision and how it might conflict with other decisions you've made. This line of strategic thought is often challenging when using archaic financial planning software that spreadsheets the data. In order to understand the strategy, one needs a centralized, observable set of outcomes which are mapped out and visual for strategic thought to occur. Dynamic Mapping is a new, more visual way of viewing such data. It might require the assistance of a Dynamic Map-certified advisor to help calculate the details of these strategic shifts and their tangible consequences, but some do-it-your-selfers will find plenty of useful information from the Dynamic Map app, from which they can make their own strategic decisions.

Whatever the reason for your interest in a book on real estate investing, I invite you to learn from the expert authors found here in Money Matters Top Tips Real Estate Edition. These tenured advisors will save you time and heartache by sharing the lessons they have learned over the years so you don't have to live through that painful learning curve. As you come to a conclusion on investment strategy, I invite you to revisit your financial plan each year by entering new and real data (not projected outcomes) based on your results. The Dynamic Map app can be found on the iOS and Android app stores and is a free download. Should you decide you need the assistance of a DM-certified advisor, please send an email to info@realintelligence360.com and I will be certain to connect you with one of these elite financial planners. Best of luck to you as you explore the opportunities, execute the strategies, and reap the rewards of real estate investing!

Jeffrey Mount

CHAPTER 1

MY FIRST MULTIFAMILY REAL ESTATE DEAL

By **ADAM TORRES**

You always remember your first. Though many years have passed since this acquisition, it seems like just the other day I heard those thrilling words from Jack Mounkes, my realtor in Arizona: "They accepted your offer." It was one of those "oh sh*t moments." Like the first time I went skydiving, right before jumping out of the plane I thought, *I guess I'm doing this.* Same with this piece of property.

What brought me to that point? Well, it all started with a conversation with one of my coworkers. They were doing math on properties in Phoenix, Arizona, where I lived at the time. The purchase prices were pre-2008 housing crisis prices. So, in hindsight, I was lucky the math didn't add up and my reserves, being a new college grad, didn't amount to much. I still wanted in the game though. So, I figured I'd make a plan.

My plan was simple. I'd spend my weekends driving by properties I'd like to own and study the market. I must have driven by 200+ properties over the course of the next year and a half. This process was an invaluable experience. While walking the properties, I met some of the owners and realtors who were showing the properties randomly. I humbly let them know I was still building my nest egg and was looking to buy in the future. Many took a liking to me and began offering advice and unique insight into the properties, such as the common issues with certain types of buildings and roof considerations. I didn't know it at the time, but I was becoming an expert in the four-plex niche in Phoenix.

During that time, I had a lucky break. For those of you reading this, just remember there are winners and losers in every deal. My lucky break was the 2008 housing crisis. Before you throw this book out the window, just remember, I was a recent college grad just starting out. So, with property values plummeting, I was finally in the game. Properties that were once selling for $250,000-$500,000 were now available as "short sell" opportunities being discounted upward of 50% from their original listing prices. Because I had done so much of the pre-work and walked hundreds of properties, I was ready to make offers.

I had to figure out the financing first. Because I'd worked for my employer for two years, had good credit, and a decent debt-to-income ratio, I was able to use traditional financing. Four-unit properties could be financed just like a regular home. I would live in one unit and rent out the other three. Even as an inexperienced real estate investor who didn't know how to run a property, I figured if everything went wrong at least I'd still have a place to stay. If everything went right, then I'd have a free place to stay and - even better - I'd get paid to live there due to being cash flow positive.

Once financing was figured out, I had to reevaluate the market. Even though I'd been walking properties for years, now everything was on sale. To take a pulse on the niche I'd picked, I picked 100 properties to walk. Some of the properties I remembered and they were like old friends welcoming me back. Strange to say, but as I was developing mastery in my niche, it seemed like I could feel the investments talking to me. After walking the 100 properties over the course of a month, doing 20+ a day on the weekends, it was time to tour the properties officially. I picked my top 15 properties and had Jack set up times to finally explore what the insides of these buildings looked like.

Walking a property on the outside versus getting into the building was a completely new experience. Some of the properties I thought were amazing from the outside were disasters on the inside. Having a limited budget and no real construction relationships in Phoenix, I knew the place I'd eventually acquire had to need little to no work. Not to mention, this was a "side hustle," so anything I did on the properties would need to be relegated to the weekends. After seeing the insides of these places, doubt definitely began to creep in. What was I getting myself into? I hadn't so much as picked up a paintbrush in years. You could say college spoiled me. Did I really want to be in this business? Was it worth the free rent?

Jack was encouraging and kept working with me. He has been an investor and realtor since after college and accumulated his own real estate portfolio over time. His guidance was invaluable and his vantage point more mature than mine. He said, "Adam, if I could finance a deal like you are with traditional financing, I'd take 50 of these fourplexes right now." With his support, we kept marching on.

After touring the properties, we had about five that we determined were within my budget and experience level, so we decided to make offers. Talk about exciting. I was so scared to make the decision, but sometimes you just have to jump out the plane and pray the parachute opens or you'll never know. Since all of the offers were on short sales, banks typically prefer cash buyers. The buyer writes a check and closes. Simple. Since I was using financing, I wasn't the exact type that banks were falling over themselves with to do business. The first two deals fell flat. A cash buyer outbid me on the first one. Talk about sad; to me, it was like someone stole my number-one draft pick. I kept thinking it wasn't fair. The second deal fell through because of some issues the bank had with the current owner of the property and wasn't necessarily an issue with me. But I lost it either way.

Feeling quite depressed at this point from the rejection and playing the waiting game, finally, we received word on my third draft pick. They accepted my offer! I drove back to the property that same day to just see if it was the right move. Was I really going to own this property? I told Jack, that it looked like I had my first player on the team. It seemed like this would be a happy ending. Well, my chaos was just beginning.

Let's talk about a mess. As I write this well over a decade later, I'm still cringing. Because of the financing involved, an appraisal had to be done and the bank would only lend based on strict standards. The appraisal was a disaster. I learned a really important lesson: Never let the tenants talk to the appraiser. As the appraiser asked the tenants what they'd liked fixed, they literally walked the appraiser through the place showing them every leak and issue with their apartments. Needless to say, my deal was hanging on by a thread. The thread was just my hope and determination.

The list of things that had to be fixed before the bank would close is too long for this chapter, but I'll give you some of the highlights. We knew there would be problems in the apartments which needed to be fixed. If you've ever bought an apartment building, normally tenants aren't exactly happy when a property changes hands, because their rents tend to go up. But I needed their cooperation to access the property and make repairs. The seller gave me permission to make the repairs, but I had a very short window to do it, as he had other offers. I was given around 10 days to make about 20-30 problems "go away" and to have the appraiser come back out. Even the appraiser apologized, saying the repairs couldn't be done that quickly and that there would be other properties in my future.

So, I had thousands of dollars of repairs and a deposit on the line. If I didn't close on time, I would lose my deposit money and the money for the repairs. Sh*t. Why was I doing this again?

Issue by issue, I chipped away at the list. Some of which were just dumb luck that it worked out. For example, the leak in the roof. It was able to be patched and didn't need to be replaced immediately, which I got in writing from the roofer. That was the main issue keeping me up at night. Then, the deal-breaker happened. In every deal, I'm told there is one thing that is unforeseen and impossible to predict but means the difference between success and failure. For me, it was a leak in a bathtub.

Apparently, the bedroom closet which shared a wall with the bathroom had mold and a leak. Oh, no! I thought it was just a leak from the tub but it was in the wall. Disaster. Impossible to fix as the time was basically up, with only two days left. Extreme measures had to be taken. I had to find a temporary solution to at least get me through the appraisal, knowing that once I had the property in my possession I'd have to do a more permanent fix. The solution was to tear out all the carpet in the bedroom, repaint the wall, caulk the tub to stop some of the leaks, and pray. Remember, this is a fully inhabited apartment!

There were even young kids running around. Also, I couldn't just rip up the carpet and leave bare concrete. It had to be recarpeted and up to the standard that the appraiser saw the first time. These were older places, so ripping up a floor is like rolling the dice.

It was a Friday afternoon when the carpet guy came to give me a quote. I booked him for the next day to install. He asked me how the floor would be prepped in such a short amount of time and how many workers I had. I told him I had my right and left hand and I'd see him the next afternoon to install, as the appraiser was coming the following day. I made him assure me they would show up and install. At this time, I'd been up for a really long time and probably looked slightly psycho and he made it very apparent they weren't interested in killing my deal. The work would be done. For those of you reading this who have been in a similar situation, yes, the story does get worse.

After pulling up the carpet, my worse nightmare happened. There wasn't one layer of carpet and padding. No, there were many layers of carpet, padding, and linoleum. Apparently, the previous owners never pulled up the old carpet or flooring. They just piled them on top of the other. Unbelievable! While that may have worked for them, it wouldn't work for me, even as a temporary fix. Because the closet had to be new and painted and all remnants of the leak had to be gone. So, I bought the family that lived in the apartment dinner, assured them again that I didn't plan on raising the rent, and told them I'd keep the noise down as much as possible.

I still remember thinking how if I were in Michigan, where I have a support system, family, and friends, I could have just called some cousins, bought them drinks, and have the whole thing knocked out in a couple of hours. But in Phoenix, with no one to call, I was basically out of luck. Especially on a Friday night. I couldn't even hire temporary labor for the day. At this time, I was awake and working on other parts of the place for at least 10 hours. Knowing I had another 8-10 hours of hard back-breaking labor ahead of me, I gave up. Not on the project! I gave up thinking. Every journey, no matter how long, begins with a single step. Well, I made that step with the first swing of the pry bar. Working through the night, filling up wheelbarrow after wheelbarrow of debris from the demolition all by myself, I was finally finished.

The next day, when I met the carpet installers, I don't remember if I'd slept. But I do remember them being surprised it was done. As the list of items got shorter and shorter, I began to see the finish line. The appraiser came back out on Sunday, inspected everything, and gave her report and approval. She was also shocked the repairs were all done. On Monday, the financing was approved with one day to spare. For all those looking to enter the real estate game, do it. Take that first step and never stop learning. To the seasoned pros reading this who have earned their stripes in the game, I hope this made you laugh because I'm sure you can relate.

CHAPTER 2

SYNDICATION

By **BENJAMIN INMAN**

Most multifamily property deals are purchased by investors pooling their money together with a qualified sponsor(s) in what is commonly known as a "syndication."

Many believe that syndicating multifamily acquisitions is mainly reserved for the novice investor or the investor who lacks capital. This can't be further from the truth. Many high net-worth people and well-seasoned groups I personally know syndicate their acquisitions, and these individuals and groups are worth between $300MM and $1B. Do they need outside capital? Perhaps not, however, they syndicate their acquisitions because they realize the many benefits syndication provides.

Syndications are typically offered to investors in the form of a Fund Investment Opportunity, or as a Deal-Specific Investment Opportunity, and these offerings are generally made available to Accredited and Sophisticated Investors or to Institutional Capital Partners.

Why Syndicate?

There are many reasons to syndicate multifamily acquisitions and raise money from others to fund your deals. For me, it seemed like the best way to start building our family portfolio. Below are a few reasons why I recommend syndicating:

a) You can acquire three times more properties!

If you are able to raise money from others, the sky's the limit. Even if you have your own money to invest, there are only so many deals you can acquire on your own. Your ability to acquire property and build out your own portfolio is only limited by your ability to find and fund the right deals. The ability to raise money and build a database of investors is an invaluable skill to have.

b) Accountability!

The more people you have reviewing the deal, the better. No matter how accustomed you are to underwriting deals and filtering through the opportunities that come your way, it's easy to overlook certain things without realizing it. When you use your own money, no one else is holding you accountable, and it is possible you will make mistakes. It may seem uncomfortable when others question and scrutinize your underwriting, but it will serve to help verify if anything was missed and to make you a better underwriter and syndicator.

c) Monthly, Quarterly, & Annual Reporting!

Investors expect monthly or quarterly property-level reporting. You will need to provide updates and financial reports to your investors so they know what's going on. Analyzing the Profit & Loss (P&L) statements and rent rolls each month and sending out reports also helps ensure you pay more attention to the performance of the property.

Depending on the time you have available to you, I also suggest you or your property manager create weekly leasing activity reports so you can keep track of rental traffic, inquires, and unit turns. There's nothing worse than not having an answer if an investor happens to call you and ask certain questions about property performance prior to the monthly reports being finalized. There's simply no excuse for not knowing what's going on at your properties.

d) Repeat Investors!

The holy grail of syndication is having repeat investors for your deals. The only way you will have repeat investors is to take care of the investors you already have, and the way you do that is to offer good distributions and ongoing communication to your investment partners, both positive and negative. There is nothing more important to investors than receiving distributions and ongoing communication so they know their investment is safe with you.

What Steps To Take?

Finding The Deal

The first task facing the multifamily sponsor is finding a great deal. To do this, the sponsor needs to network with brokers, lenders, property managers, appraisers, attorneys, accountants, or other investors in order to keep good deal-flow. Finding a good deal is a numbers game; a sponsor needs to look at 100 different deals, analyze the financials and perform underwriting on the deals, then place offers on 10 of them in the form of a Letter-of-Intent (LOI), and may end up getting one accepted.

The Pitch Book

As you are building your track record of multifamily acquisitions, you will need to create and use a "Pitch Book" listing any past deals you have done, along with a featured live deal you have available.

A Pitch Book can be a 1 to 5-page document, or longer if you prefer. The Pitch Book is a tool you will use to present to potential investors you are hoping to attract to your deal while you are having your Private Placement Memorandum (PPM) created (more on this later in the chapter).

A Pitch Book typically contains property-level specifics including, but not limited to, actual photos, location information, property financials, rent roll, and projected investor returns, as well as information about the fact that you have this particular deal under contract. In other words, you approach your potential investors with a summary that presents an active deal you have control of and it will need to align with your yet-to-be-created PPM.

The main goal is to get verbal capital commitments early on, or at least start building out your relationship database of potential investors. It's never too early to start building your list of investors. Trust me on this! To this day, I always make sure I have business cards, along with a digital or physical Pitch Book I can send immediately to anyone I meet. Whether it's a planned meeting or an unplanned meeting that happens unexpectedly, you should always be ready to strike when the iron is hot!

Benefits of a Pitch Book:
- A Pitch Book forces you to know your deal inside and out. Seeing the photos, touring the property, and talking about it more and more will make the deal real for you. The more real the deal is to you, the more comfortable you will be and the more confidently you will talk about it when discussing with investors.
- I have had a certain partner in some deals in the past that would need me on calls to help him walk his investors through a deal we were co-sponsoring together, and I was constantly blown away by how little he actually knew. You simply cannot

be effective without knowing your deal top to bottom, inside and out.

- A Pitch Book provides an opportunity to speak with your investors. You should begin scheduling meetings with investors as soon as possible and letting them know you have an active deal you would like for them to consider investing in. Then you hand them or email them your Pitch Book and ask for feedback.

- A Pitch Book is a tool to help attain capital commitments from investors. As soon as you get a property under contract you should start reaching out to your database of investors. As you move through your Due Diligence period, your goal should be to receive capital commitments early on from investors. Trust me when I tell you that it will help you sleep better at night.

- The last thing you want is to be scrambling around to finish out your capital raise a week before closing on a deal you have under contract. I have been there and done that! This will only create undue stress in your life and is the main reason I suggest raising capital for your deal as early in the process as possible.

- A Pitch Book helps you to continue building your investor database. It's never too early to build out your relationship database of investors. Regardless if you currently have a deal under contract, or not, I recommend continuing to build out your investor database before, during, and after your current deal. As you acquire more properties, continue to update your Pitch Book with your current owned-assets. It will serve to continue adding to your credibility and improving your track record.

- You will find that as you do this, investors who may have decided to initially pass on your offerings up to this point may now be ready to invest with you moving forward. Some investors may want to monitor your process from afar just to make sure you can and will do what you say. You never know when the tipping point will be for each investor to finally jump in with you so ALWAYS be ready.

Pitch Book Structure

Begin with creating a cover page and then on the following pages incorporate pictures and property-level information that you can borrow from the Offering Memorandum provided by the broker. The Pitch Book should include information such as photos, financials, rent roll, unit mix, information about the area, and demographics, along with your planned business strategy on how you plan to operate the property.

If you need a little inspiration you can always review the Offering Memorandum provided by the broker, or contact brokers who are marketing properties similar to yours, register for their offering(s), sign the non-disclosure agreement, and download the marketing brochure for each property. You can use these marketing brochures to help you get an idea of what you are looking to create to present to your investors.

Incorporate Your Underwriting

The Pitch Book you create should contain the actual financials (T12) of the property, along with the projected financials from the underwriting you created for the property. According to your business plan, you will need to base your underwriting on 3-10-year hold periods. I typically choose 3-7-year hold periods in my underwriting, depending on the property I am purchasing. Typically, investors will ask how long you plan on holding the property, but if they do not ask, I would let them know upfront. This will keep you from possibly having investors drop out later as they discover the hold period and conclude it is too short or too long for their needs.

You should structure the deal in such a way to achieve the desired returns for you and your investment partners. There are several scenarios here, but you could either keep it simple and use one return hurdle of something similar to a 75%/25% split of Cash Flow between you and your investors after a predetermined rate of return of something like 7%-8%, or structure a 2-3 tier waterfall structure of something like 80%/20% split of returns between you and your investors after returns from 8% up to 10%, a 75%/25% split of returns over 10% up to 12%, and then a 70%/30% split of anything above 12%.

It is very important you do your own underwriting so you will know how and why the deal works and so that you are able to intelligently speak to investors about the projected performance of your deal. If you are not able to speak intelligently about your deal and how you plan on taking it from A to Z in order to get higher rents, you will find it very difficult to raise capital from potential investors.

Assemble Your Pitch Book

These are the pages or sections your Pitch Book should contain, and I have listed them in the order in which I would place them.

Executive Summary

This section contains a summary of the investment terms you are offering to prospective investors. It will typically include information on the following:

- Preferred rate of return
- Minimum equity required from each investor
- Total equity required
- Projected return expectations
- Maximum investment amounts you are seeking from investors
- The term of the investment
- Description of the property
- Overview of the business plan
- The renovation plan for both interiors and exteriors

Property and Market-level Information

In this section, you will include a description of the property and the market where the property is located. You will also include factual information such as unit mix, unit count, in-place rents, and a snapshot of the current market rents for like-kind properties.

I would also provide more detail from the business plan and explain what other comparables in the market are doing in order to further support your business plan analysis. For example, if you are planning to do some upgrades to the interiors and exteriors of the property to further justify the proposed rent increases, that would also go in this section. If you are planning to implement a value-add strategy, I would NOT leave this detail out!

In-Place Financials

Here you will include the actual in-place profit and loss statement (P&L) and rent rolls. My suggestion is to save yourself and your investors time and frustration and make sure the P&L and rent roll line up from the start. Otherwise, your numbers may be off a little and you will need to be able to defend it.

Projections and Investor Returns

Here you should include the 3-10-year projections you are anticipating for the property, along with the expected returns you are offering the investors.

Information About You (or Your Group)

Include a bio and headshot of yourself along with any other partner you have on the sponsorship side. You can also include other members of your team like your attorney, property management partner, lender, co-sponsor (if any), etc. While any info about the sponsor and co-sponsor is not necessary, it can only help your position and prove that you are a trusted sponsor.

Information About Your Chosen Management Partner

I would include a bio of the management company you have selected to use for the property. If you do not have a bio of the management company you are planning to use, you can ask them to send you one and they will be happy to do so.

Meeting With Investors

Always have a goal when you are meeting with investors. You should always know the desired outcome of your meeting, and that desired outcome, of course, being a capital commitment. Please keep in mind, however, that you may not get a commitment from your first meeting with a potential investor. Sometimes it may take 2-3 meetings with the same investor before you get a commitment. Do not be worried, this is very common. Many times investors want to meet so they can get comfortable with you and not just the deal itself. Do not overthink this process. Just be yourself and do not try and overpitch, or oversell, the deal. You may come across as desperate and that will usually turn investors away.

Risk Factors

You need to identify the main risk factors in your offering and lay them out in your Pitch Book with how you plan to address them. Although this will be covered in your PPM, I would also mention it here. In order to get a commitment from an investor, you have to understand and address their unspoken fears, which is that they could lose part or all of their investment. It will make you more credible if you are upfront and address the potential risks head-on and lay out a clear plan of how you plan to mitigate them.

The focus is on you

If the potential investor has never invested with you before, you will likely need to sell him or her on why they should invest with you. After all, they are not just investing in the deal you are presenting, they are also investing in YOU, the sponsor. They have risk in you as well, and you will need to help them understand why you are worth the investment. Focus on building a genuine rapport with your investor(s), because it would be a good idea to build strong trust with him or her if you plan to have them around for future deals.

I would plan on spending most of the first or second meeting making the investor comfortable with you and not only the deal itself. Once you relieve the investor of any concerns they may have about you, only then can you address any objections about the deal itself.

After you briefly go through your personal life, I would immediately go into describing your professional background. Keep a heavy focus on and describe any track record you may have in doing this for others and/or how your prior success in a different field will help you achieve your goals in the particular deal you are presenting.

Structuring the Opportunity

How the opportunity you are presenting to investors is structured depends on the complexity of the investment. There are several options and you, together with your attorney, can decide what's best for your situation. Regardless of the option, you should purchase the property in the name of an LLC or LP. I recommend naming an entity that is more logical to the exact deal, e.g., the name of the property with the unit count at the end OR the name of the property with "equity partners" at the end, e.g., Crestview Apartments 100, LLC., or Crestview Apartments Equity Partners, LLC.

Purchasing the property in the name of an LLC protects your personal assets and other business assets. If the business were to fail, or for some reason and your LLC is sued, then the suit is limited to the LLC, not to the other assets you control.

Creating an LLC is a relatively straightforward process you can usually do online. However, I strongly suggest having your attorney or CPA guide you, since the process differs slightly by state. You will generally need to do the following (depending on your state):

- Search for an available name, complete an application, and pay a fee. (Do an online search for "How to register an LLC in [your state]").
- Obtain a Federal Tax ID for the LLC (EIN Numbers), which you can do on the IRS website. Go to www.irs.gov and look for "Apply for an Employer Identification Number (EIN)."
- In some jurisdictions, you may need to apply for a business license.
- Create the Operating Agreement for your LLC.
- Using your LLC and EIN, you can open a business bank account.

Registering an LLC and paying an attorney to draft documents costs money, so do this only after you have a property secured and you're confident you are moving forward with the purchase of the property. When you make offers, list the buyer in the contract as "Entity Yet to be Created," or you can use your name as a placeholder and then assign the contract to your new entity once it's ready. Your attorney should be familiar with this process, so don't be overly concerned with this step. Most sellers, like most attorneys, will also be very accustomed to this process.

The Operating Agreement is usually several pages long. I would recommend using one that defines who is allowed to make what decisions, what process is to be followed for these decisions to be made, and how people can be added or removed from the LLC, among other details.

You can usually download an Operating Agreement from LegalZoom.com, but I would recommend having your attorney create one for you from scratch which is specific to your unique needs. A competent attorney will charge you to create an operating agreement, and depending on the complexity, I would ask for a proposed cost before agreeing. The LLC is a separate entity from you and any partners, and the Operating Agreement should clearly define how your LLC is governed. Operating Agreements give you credibility with your partners and will provide the proper protection if needed.

The operating agreement should define the ownership percentages of each member and how profits are to be distributed. It also defines other details, such as the end of the fiscal year and when and where the annual member meeting will be held.

You can usually structure the LLC in several different ways using the Operating Agreement.

Below are two examples:
1. You as Sole Member of your LLC IF you are borrowing money from investors. In this structure, you are borrowing cash from investors who get a promissory note secured against the building.
2. Multiple member LLC. In this structure, your investors/partners are contributing capital for a percentage of the deal. Each investor is a "member" of the LLC, and members, including you, may or may not have equal voting rights (depending on how your Operating Agreement is structured). The operating agreement defines what things you can do as a manager without requiring a vote by the other members.

Using the Operating Agreement, you can give your partners, and/or investors no decision-making authority or you can give them more authority. The Operating Agreement should also define how additional capital can be raised at a later time if needed, or how investors' can be bought out.

Security Laws. Any time you receive funds from others, you are effectively selling shares, or securities, in the LLC (the entity) that will actually own the property. As such, this falls under securities laws, which should be followed closely. I do NOT recommend that you try and navigate the securities waters without the assistance of an experienced attorney. This is an area I do not take chances on, and to this day I still use the same attorney to create my Private Placement Memorandums (PPM).

The securities laws differ by state. Generally, you will need to provide investors who are interested in investing with you a disclosure document they will need to sign, and you may need to file certain forms with your state and/or the SEC. In addition, if you have three investors who are all from different states and each of them is investing in a specific property with you in your state, you may have to also file in each of their respective states. If you decide to use an attorney that specializes in creating Private Placement Memorandums (PPM), I would also recommend having the same attorney file the necessary documents on your behalf with each state and the SEC, if required.

While it's not difficult to comply with state and SEC securities laws, it will cost money, because a securities attorney will need to advise you and prepare the Private Placement Memorandum (PPM) according to your unique needs. This will usually cost between $6,500 to $20,000 depending on the size and complexity of the offering. In my experience, however, my costs have typically been in the $7,500-$15,000 range, depending on whether I am having the attorney that is drafting the PPM also draft the Operating Agreements.

Why issue a Private Placement Memorandum (PPM)?

The purpose of the PPM is to disclose all potential risks of the investment to your investors and to ultimately protect you, the sponsor. If you don't issue a PPM and something bad happens to the deal, your investors could contact your state's Securities and Exchange Commission (SEC) and file a complaint against you. The SEC will usually investigate the complaint and the first thing they'll check is to see if the offering was registered with the proper disclosures. If you did not register your offering, the SEC can prosecute and/or fine you.

Typically included in the PPM, investors get a Subscription Agreement. The purpose of the Subscription Agreement is for the investor to agree to the investment amount, acknowledge the receipt of the PPM, and make other required disclosures to comply with SEC regulations.

Although others may try and discourage you from having a PPM drafted by a qualified attorney in order to avoid the added costs, I would highly recommend that you have PPMs created for your first several deals.

Consult with your legal counsel, as I am not an attorney.

CHAPTER 3

DE-CON-STRUCT-ING THE LAW OF CONSTRUCTION FOR CALIFORNIA REAL ESTATE INVESTORS & DEVELOPERS

By **GARRETT M. MOTT, ESQ.**

Before they came to me, if you asked any of my real estate investor clients what an HPOZ is or how to serve a three-day notice, they would have confidently shared their answers. But what if you'd asked them about after they paid their contractor the next installment payment if their contractor issued an unconditional waiver and release? "A what?" they would exclaim.

Virtually every developer deals with construction defect claims throughout their entrepreneurial career. But when new clients inevitably come to me, the first question I ask is, for them, completely unexpected: "Is the project new construction or a remodel?" And then there is the one ubiquitous (and distressing) issue that everyone has heard of, but very few understand: change orders.

This primer provides a fundamental introduction to the three most common, yet unfamiliar, issues for real estate investors and developers: mechanic's liens, the Right to Repair Act, and change orders.

Mechanic's Liens

Despite the name, a "mechanics' lien" is a type of legal claim against a property used by contractors, subcontractors, and materials suppliers to stake a claim against real property that has been improved, but for which no payment has been made. For example, if a real estate investor remodels two bathrooms in his latest duplex purchase, and the subcontractor plumber who installed the tubs was not paid by the general contractor, under the right circumstances, a lien can be placed against the investor's house to recover the money. Mechanic's liens are a particularly sore spot for investors and developers because if one is recorded against a property, it can critically frustrate efforts to sell the property in a timely manner.

The three basic topics relating to mechanic's liens investors and developers need to know are preliminary notices, waiver and release forms, and lien release bonds.

As to the first, the so-called "prelim" is a notice served on the owner, general contractor (GC), and construction lender, if any, which informs them that the one serving the notice is providing services or material to the project. The purpose of the prelim is to inform the owner (in our case) that a subcontractor or materials supplier, who the owner likely does not know, is working on the job. All claimants who are not directly contracting with the owner must serve a prelim to be protected by mechanic's lien law. This is critically important and few subcontractors and materials suppliers follow this law's strictures. Indeed, I have had clients who did not know the rules get into lengthy settlement negotiations over wrongly-recorded mechanic's liens made by subcontractors who never served a prelim. If they had known that a mechanic's lien is invalid without a prelim, they would have appreciated their superior negotiating position.

As to the waiver and release forms, while few use them right, if you run your project using them, you will seldom have disputes about payment. These waivers, when executed by the claimant (general contractor, subcontractor, or materials supplier), act to release any lien rights by the claimant. The law provides four types of waivers and the procedure for their use: the (1) conditional and (2) unconditional waivers and release upon progress payment, and the (3) conditional and (4) final waivers and release upon final payment. You can find fillable forms here: http://www.cslb.ca.gov/Consumers/ Legal_Issues_For_Consumers/Mechanics_Lien/Conditional_And_ Unconditional_Waiver_Release_Form.aspx

How does the process work? First, insist on your contract with the GC (in the industry, we call it the "prime contract") include that the GC and its subcontractors provide you with a conditional waiver and release upon progress payment with each progress invoice. That way, when a particular construction milestone is reached under the contract (say, rough plumbing) the contractor and its subcontractors should provide you with a conditional waiver and release upon progress payment. Then, after payment is made for that milestone, insist the contractor provide you with an unconditional waiver and release upon progress payment. This process repeats until the final payment. For the final payment, the contractor should first issue a conditional waiver and release upon final payment, triggering you, the owner, to pay. After final payment is made, insist via the contract that the contractor and its subcontractors provide you with a final waiver and release upon final payment. While this process appears tedious, effectively managing it can essentially eliminate the risk of a mechanic's lien being recorded against your property.

Lastly, if despite your efforts, a mechanic's lien is recorded against the property and the timing of the sale is critical, consider utilizing a lien release bond. A lien release bond is a pot of money that you, the real estate investor/developer, replace with the claimant's mechanic lien rights to your property. That way, the claimant can go after the money, instead of your property. The lien release bond clears the title, freeing you to sell the property unencumbered. To obtain a lien release bond, contact a surety company, who will provide you with underwriting and bond execution. Like with most binary choices in life, unencumbering the property comes at a price: the bond must be in an amount 125 percent the amount of claim and the claimant has six months to sue on the bond (where the claimant normally has only 90 days to do so with real property).

The Right to Repair Act

The Right to Repair Act (also known fondly as "SB800") is California's attempt to provide prelitigation dispute resolution procedures for construction defect claims relating to new residential construction. Those naturally concerned with SB800 are owner-builders who develop new condominium complexes or housing tracks. While there are a number of rules and timelines, we'll concern ourselves here with two common legal issues that arise in SB800 cases: the economic loss rule and the statute of limitations.

Here's a little law school Torts 101: The economic loss rule provides that a party who suffers only economic harm may recover damages for that harm based only upon a contractual claim and not on a tort theory, such as negligence or strict liability. The reason this is important is that prior to SB800, tort claims (mainly ones of negligence) concerning residential construction defects were often barred because the defects only caused economic loss. After SB800, owner-builders have tort liability to homeowners (of course, the Act's prelitigation dispute resolution procedures must first be exhausted). This is because the Act establishes a set of standards for residential construction which includes everything from moisture barriers on windows to substrate sheathing and framing. See Cal. Civil Codes §§ 896, 897.

Let's continue our law school primer with a little Civil Procedure 101: A "statute of limitation" is a law that sets the maximum time after an event within which a legal proceeding may be initiated. Most owner-builders know of one specific statute of limitations, called the 10-year rule, which provides that claims relating to latent construction defects be brought within 10 years. SB800 created a whole new statute of limitations paradigm that often trips up homeowners.

For example, the statute of limitations for fit and finish of flooring, paint, trim, countertops, and exterior walls is just one (1) year from the close of escrow. Knowing these and the other intricate requirements of SB800 is critical if you are an owner-builder of new residential construction.

Change Orders

It is a rare case indeed when construction relating to a real estate investment property does not involve a change from the bid set of plans. For that reason, every real estate investor and developer should understand what a change order is and how to manage the eventual disputes relating to them. A "change order" is the industry term for a modification to a construction contract which changes the contractor's scope of work. As a classic example, suppose an owner seeks to move the location of a retaining wall on the plans to accommodate some design elements, like a new trellised arcade. The contractor will issue a change order for the amount outside the scope of the original work to perform the new work. Herein lies the rub: because the contractor is already on the job and because of the sunken cost fallacy, the owner, who now has less leverage on the project, feels compelled to pay whatever amount the change order costs. This process often leads to a breakdown in trust, inefficiencies on the job, and sometimes significant project delays.

Here are two tips to avoid this scenario:

1. The construction contract needs to contain two provisions: one provision that contains the procedure for changes and an "order-of-precedence clause" that determines whether the specifications or drawings control. As to the procedure, I have seen the effective use of contracts where the architect, who is hired by the owner, oversees each proposed change order. I have also seen effective use of third-party estimators or outside contractors for particularly large change orders, who provide the owner with an estimate of the extra work to be used in negotiation with the project's contractor. Using these techniques shifts the leverage back to the owner.

2. Require change orders to be in writing. The change order process should be that the contractor prepares a change order proposal that sets out the price for extra work, and then the owner and contractor negotiate over scope, price, and schedule. Then, a written change order is prepared and signed by the parties, and thereafter, the contractor begins work. This process is rarely followed; often contractors proceed with doing extra work without first obtaining a signed change order and owners go along with it. This "course of dealing" can lead to situations where field changes are made

and the owner is still bound, despite the contract requiring otherwise. To avoid this, stick to the contract.

Each of the above issues is widespread and thus their workings are vital for you to understand. Hopefully, this primer has elevated your knowledge (and confidence) of these subjects from "I've heard of that..." to "I know what we should do."

CHAPTER 4

ART MEETS REAL ESTATE

By **HARLAN GLEESON**

As a kid, I got to watch The Empire Strikes Back on one of the editing machines rented out by my dad's company, The Eagle Eye Film Company. When my dad wasn't renting out editing equipment, he was acting in movies. My mother was a multimedia artist who led by example for her 10 children more than her words. I have sought my entire life to speak through my actions and less through my words in honor of my mother's consistent presence. Through both of my parents, I came to love and appreciate true art that stands on content and style alone.

I was a teenager living in the inner-city neighborhood of Koreatown, Los Angeles, experiencing life and having fun with my friends as any young teenager would. As if overnight, the neighborhood changed when the crack cocaine epidemic hit the streets of Los Angeles. Very suddenly, it scrambled everything around me. The whole vibe in the inner-city was sketchy, dark, and desperate. I saw people struggle with addiction and it hit close to home, touching the lives of my older brothers and their closest friends. Gangs, of course, had been a part of Los Angeles culture for over 100 years, but with the onslaught of the drugs and money, gang culture hit an apex in the '80s. I wanted no part of that madness. Thankfully, I did not get hooked on crack or any other drugs and didn't join the gang culture fold. I saw so much senseless violence and destructive drug abuse and it turned my stomach. My friends and I were open to finding our place in the world when one of our moms brought us out to see the newly minted New York movie, Wild Style. A movie set squarely in the burgeoning East Coast graffiti art and hip hop culture, it rendered a fascinating world. When the credits rolled, all of us knew this was for us. We immediately learned how to breakdance and embraced our new lives as street artists. I and my group of friends started up our crew and called it KGB, an acronym for Kids Gone Bad.

Like all of the plot twists in my life, graffiti was a colorful and unexpected turn. First, it put me squarely into criminal behavior. For right or wrong, I saw it as a victimless crime, a kind of beneficial creative vandalism that kept me out of the drugs and violence occurring all around me. That was a wonderful thing. Second, graffiti channeled my rebellion and gave me an expressive outlet to create something exciting on the blank walls of our otherwise drab neighborhood. It gave my friends and me deep satisfaction. We were not vandal taggers, we were creative street artists. When we found the right wall, we would paint something meaningful and beautiful.

We were part of the pioneering first wave of street art and through our hard work and dedication, we became respected. Unlike the gang wars all around us, our "wars" were fought with paint. Our victories were achieved by bringing artistic innovation and power to life through careful planning and teamwork. Designing, executing, and evading capture were the foremost priorities. There were many close calls and a few arrests. That never stopped us. The art continued to flow from our creative spirit through our spray cans onto the city walls.

My first arrest was for vandalizing in the city of San Francisco. My parents contacted their friend to bail me and a friend out of jail. We got a long lecture by our San Francisco savior (a wonderful African-American jazz musician) to keep up our artwork but "bring it out without getting into trouble and needing to get bailed out of jail!" We were humbled and dreaded our return to L.A. to face the wrath of our parents. My father - ever with the Irish humor - celebrated our arrests by making us t-shirts which read, "I left my art in San Francisco." Owing in part to my three older brothers and the trouble they had given my parents, and partially to support my creative impulses, they went easy on me. I, for my part, was undaunted. I continued my quest to get better and better, seizing every opportunity to bring colors and life to walls. I and the crew would scope out the perfect wall, look for escape routes, and plan our piece. We would spend the night at a friend's house nearby and sneak out to pull off our artistic vandalism. There was an efficiency to our work, as each person knew their assignment. We wasted zero time delivering our wonders to the public. The tone was very serious when it came to our projects.

We all came to understand that our art required a certain amount of operational complexity, tempered by a willingness to be bold, gritty, and also faithful. Graffiti art pieces, like any business enterprises or creative projects, have a mysterious process all their own. You can see this sometimes unwieldy process unfold in the movie Wild Style. Zoro, the protagonist in the movie, had been struggling with his epic graffiti art piece, when his girlfriend, lady Pink, in a stroke of brilliance, related something to him which clarified his vision and gave the meaning and direction to his art he needed. We learned, like Zoro, that the artist must always make space for the muse to play. With artwork, meaning can be derived in overt, as well as covert currents and undercurrents, with direct and metaphorical expressions. True, we were street artists, but that didn't mean we weren't thinking with the subtlety of the greats. You plan to your best ability and then you trust that the process of execution will deliver, and that, when needed, the magic muse will arrive just in time. It always, always did.

After high school, I got my degree in history and chose a career in computer hardware sales. The money was excellent and creating and operating a business gave full expression to other aspects of my creative spirit. Possessing the entrepreneurial passion, I formed my own company, naming it after the street I grew up on - Kingsley Drive - and embracing my connection and affection for the neighborhood. Kingsley Computers became 20 years of my life. Graffiti art had taught me well, actually. Plan, think everything through to the best of your ability and then execute with full commitment. Let the work speak for itself. I came to find it was a winning equation in business. Most of my family members - there are 10 kids in my family - worked at the company at one time or another. I was happy to provide them all with opportunities when they needed them.

I never quit being a graffiti artist. I continued thinking about themes for my art and never stopped painting. I just ceased doing it illegally. I painted one or two pieces a month and on the side, I bought and sold art as a collector and investor. While I was in the computer business, I adorned my walls with some of the most talented artists I knew. They were always looking for walls to hang their art where it would be seen. My office walls transformed our corporate space in new and exciting ways, and I experienced firsthand the impact our commitment to art had on the quality of life for all who came through our space. All of my clients and friends loved coming to my offices. I became famous in the computer industry for my office and its art collection.

After 20 years in computers, I decided to dedicate myself full time to the world of art - bringing the Los Angeles brand of creativity to the professional world in new ways. I have dived in with both feet, taking wonderful L.A. artists I grew up with - as well as artists I am currently getting to know - to professional spaces and splashing their art on office walls. A win-win, giving the artist an avenue to greater exposure and introducing really talented, original creative work to the professional wall space. I am using my many years of experience in the art world and employing my business expertise to blend my artist friends with my corporate professional colleagues.

Through direct sales, leased art, and even pop-up galleries, I am bringing a new, direct technique to a market as old as the commerce of art itself. The art I love is making its way around the city I love. As a kid, I used to travel the streets of Los Angeles looking for the good walls, ones that would be just the right fit for the KGB crew's graffiti artwork. I am doing the same thing now, only inside and outside of corporate spaces. I bring my passion and eye for art to consulting with my clients to hang that perfect piece - matching the clients' needs for their space with the artists and their work.

I know I am not alone in noticing the many spaces around the city which need art curation. Without art expertise, many of these spaces are lost opportunities for the corporate set to elevate their workspaces with great West Coast art. To hang something exciting, a piece that challenges the viewer and puts them in touch with something just beyond their understanding, all with the local and dynamic art of L.A. is my number one mission. Art should arrest your senses and trigger a response for its witness to want to know more about it. I have seen, firsthand, passionate conversations between my clients and their customers and employees about the artwork on their walls. The pieces immediately create a basis for meaningful discussions and bonding experiences. These are the results I work very very hard for.

For my work, I am constantly connecting with as many artists as possible, and some in my stable go back to my youth. I understand the artists' dedication and commitment to their craft and have a deep respect for what it takes to produce really good work. I go through much the same process when recommending art as the artist goes through while creating it. I have deep confidence in my instincts and invariably find just the right fit. One that pushes internal growth by investigating personal aesthetic boundaries. The conversations I have with my clients about art often takes us back to their memories of their victories and defeats, lost loves, future goals, and even intense struggles - the art prompts deep reflection. Art is always about creating opportunities for its subject at personal reflection. Reflections that can inspire inner growth and emotional evaluation. Art is rendered for us to see in it our own experiences and give us a chance at a kind of catharsis. Art has immense power and life in it and we are all deeply enriched by it. I aim for this experience for my clients and have been rewarded with success as a result.

So, if you are currently sitting in your office eight to ten hours a day and you are looking at blank walls or mass-produced art, know that you can do better by tapping into the vast and culturally rich world of the Los Angeles art scene. You can have a gallery all your own right where you work.

Simply send an email or make a telephone call and begin the conversation.

CHAPTER 5

LEADERSHIP IS SERVICE

By **JAMES HUANG**

Servant Leadership is so very important to successfully run any organization. What do I mean by "servant leadership"? It's where, as a leader, you put others before yourself; you put the organization, its leaders, and its members first, while you are at the end, steering the ship.

I've always been a strong believer in this type of leadership. It's more than just leading by example and showing that you mean what you say and can walk the walk. It's about **being open, transparent, and accountable to the people you serve.** It's about helping your peers and employees become the best they can be, even if that means they will become better then you. Because as a business or an organization, we win or lose as a team. In my leadership quest, I want those who know me or work with me to be able to say that while I am not perfect, I practice what I preach and I will always try my best and learn from my mistakes. I wake up each day a better person than the day before.

I want to always learn from my mistakes and grow; I'm a fighter and I will go down fighting for the people and business I serve.

In 2003, I founded BRC Advisors, a full-service commercial real estate company. We grew to five offices and over 150 agents, with property management, syndication/finance, and other lines of business before the Great Recession struck. One day I thought life was set and I could retire early and the next day, my life was turned upside-down. We had no cash flow, no new deals, creditors were hounding me, and all of my employees were panicking.

It would have been easier to give up, let go, and figure out something new for myself. To let my partners and employees fend for themselves and just focus on myself.

Instead, I had to get on my knees and pray and call on my inner strength to fight through the worst of times and work my hardest to keep the company together. I have never been so humbled or so vulnerable as during that time, and I was willing to humble myself if that was what it took.

One example that comes to mind is when I was on the phone with the Voice Over IP company. We were four months behind on our bill and they were going to shut off our phone systems, which would have put us out of business. I begged the accounts payable department not to shut off our phones and promised I'd pay them as soon as any money came into the business.

During that time, we made almost no money, but I had $120,000 in rent, payroll, and all the expenses of running a business. The accounts payable person moved me up the food chain, and I eventually found myself on a call with the president of the phone company. In a spectacular coincidence, the president was someone I'd worked with years before at Dean Witter Reynolds, a stock brokerage and securities firm. We hadn't spoken in a long time, but he remembered me. He said, "I'll tell you what I'll do. I will wipe out your debt, give you six months free, and then you start paying again starting in the seventh month. Pay it consistently and let me know if you have a problem. Don't embarrass me or let me down, and please keep in touch if there are any issues."

A man I hadn't spoken to in close to 10 years remembered me and thought enough of me to help me in my time of need. As I said, I'm not perfect, but I know I was working hard and a fighter even then. Always do your best because you don't know who may be watching.

Renegotiating my phone bill and even other bills were not enough to get BRC Advisors back on its feet or through the worst of it, and I was forced to ask for help from friends, agents, and employees. Every single one of them simply said, "How much do you need?" I had to ask my agents to delay their commission checks and lend that money to the company for an undetermined amount of time; every one of them yes.

The entire time, I stayed open and transparent with my employees. I knew they were afraid of being laid off and I was honest that layoffs might be necessary unless they were willing to take a pay cut. Each one said they would take a pay cut to keep everyone there.

So many people chose to stick with me and help get the company through the recession. I believe that to have good friends, one must first BE a good friend. Just as to have great employees, one must be a great employee and a leader who puts their needs above his own. I've lived by this principle throughout my life. Friendship is something to be cherished more than material goods. You are truly wealthy when you have good friends.

We made it through the recession and came out the other side thriving. In 2015, BRC merged with Sperry Commercial Global Affiliates (www.sperrycga.com), and I am the President of it. By going through the worst time in my life and business with the help of others, I found my true passion: helping people.

As a servant leader, that is my ultimate goal. It's all about the people around you. If they prosper, so do you and the business, which means you can do more good for society and the community you live in.

Part of that is consulting with companies to help them connect with the tools, resources, and people they need to grow, scale, and thrive. I aim to use everything I've learned to help the people around me. My business dream is to be the first minority to run a top-10 commercial real estate brokerage firm in the U.S., and to create opportunities and pipelines for women and underserved communities not currently represented in this industry.

Purpose

Everyone needs to find a purpose bigger than ourselves to strive and work toward. I am now able to use my experiences and success to help people and live the "American dream."

I am the 2020 National President of AREAA (www.areaa.org), where our mission is sustainable homeownership for Asian Americans, Pacific Islanders, and all communities, especially for underserved groups and being a powerful national voice for housing issues that affect our communities. When my parents immigrated to the U.S., their "American dream" was to become citizens and raise a family in the land of opportunity. Another element of the American dream is homeownership. To many, owning a home represents wealth, prosperity, family, and financial security. I work toward that with my own company and through AREAA.

Entrepreneurship is also an American dream; to want to start a business that can grow into a national or international business recognized around the world. Small businesses are the backbone of this country and I want to help entrepreneurs learn how to start, grow and scale their businesses. In doing so, we create more jobs and opportunities, which helps others and builds stronger communities.

Servant Leadership

In the 18th century, King Frederick of Prussia called himself "the first servant of the state," and in 1970, Robert K. Greenleaf popularized "servant leadership" in an essay titled "The Servant as Leader." He credited Herman Hesse's 1932 book *Journey to the East* as inspiration.

Servant leadership creates a sense of community and builds trust in an organization, which leads to higher employee retention, better morale, and innovation. It involves the leader being openly communicative, having empathy and awareness of others, and a deep commitment to the growth and success of others.

"The servant-leader is a servant first. It begins with the natural feeling that one wants to serve, to serve first." - Robert K. Greenleaf

How can you implement servant leadership into your company and put your people first?

You do so by listening to the needs of your employees and peers, acknowledging their perspectives, giving them support to reach their goals, being transparent, and demonstrating your own persistence.

Listening

It's not about simply hearing someone's opinions or ideas. It's about purposeful listening, active listening, and engaged listening. Every single person has value and deserves trust and respect, and listening to them asking for their participation and feedback is key. Make sure to avoid interrupting them and listening to what they have to say, even when you don't ultimately implement their ideas.

Acknowledgment

Acknowledge your employees' hard work and persistence and model those traits yourself. Take the time to encourage innovation, creativity, and employees taking action. Make sure to also acknowledge that no one is perfect and mistakes happen.

Support

Provide guidance and support to your employees and peers, and make sure your company has the tools and resources your employees need to do their jobs well. Listen to what they need and do your best to provide it. Happy employees are ones who are getting their needs met and feel supported in their role.

Transparency

Servant leaders understand that everyone makes mistakes, and they acknowledge their own, too. They are open with their employees about what is happening with the company and don't hide decisions behind multiple layers of management. Honesty is an important aspect of building trust.

Persistence

Good servant leaders are determined and persistent in reaching their goals and lead by example. They encourage others to be tenacious and persistent when working toward their goals, too. Encourage your employees to dream big and work hard, and also to strive to value others' ideas and perspectives.

Summary

In the worst time in my business, I was able to trust and rely on those around me, be transparent and open with my team, and work hard to get through it. I learned that it was bigger than me alone and that every small win makes a difference and leads to bigger wins. Because of that experience and other obstacles in life, I have learned that while being a servant leader sometimes requires sacrifice, it also comes with great rewards. Every day I continue to grow and try to help others so that we can all be stronger.

CHAPTER 6

INVESTING IS FOR RICH PEOPLE

By **JEFF MOUNT & MIKE HELGESEN**

"Investing is for rich people. We are not, and will never be, one of them. You will never be able to truly retire." These were the flawed 'words of wisdom' given to me by my parents and friends when I was growing up. Growing up lower-middle-class means you live paycheck to paycheck. It means your family is vulnerable to the risk vortex (a term often used in the Dynamic Map financial planning method), which includes illness, injury, unexpected layoffs that precede long periods of unemployment, and other unforeseen events that cause a financial catastrophe.

People who constrain future entrepreneurs, future captains of industry, and future real estate moguls with such garbage are toxic and their influence can often suppress greatness. Although I shy away from the word 'great,' I was one of the fortunate ones who escaped the constant bombardment of pessimism. Moving away from that poisonous environment and into a wealthy community after college encouraged me to seek out financial literacy and build a life of significance. I am pleased to say that my children will never have to endure the pessimism that came from the community I endured when I was a child. The question now is: How do we eradicate this pessimism so everyone has a chance at greatness? Financial literacy can have a meaningful impact on the lives of those who embrace financial planning and investing wisely.

What is the cumulative effect of this pessimism? A few years ago, I participated on a local board for Junior Achievement. Their three value propositions are entrepreneurship, work readiness, and financial literacy. As a professional in the financial services industry, I felt like I had something to offer. My first real test came when I was asked to teach a high school class about the basics of credit. The course wasn't tough, but the crowd was! This high school class was in an economically devastated inner-city school in Bridgeport, Connecticut. So, here I am – a white guy in a suit trying to connect with these young people who don't see any reason to pay attention.

I tried a "rule of 72" trick to get them engaged in conversation. "Which would benefit you more, a $1 million lump sum OR one penny doubled every day for 30 days?" They loved this! We did the math and the outcome astonished them. The effect of doubling your money is incredible, especially when dealing with larger numbers. Shortly after that, I had to begin the course on the basics of credit and noticed the look of complete resignation on their faces. I asked who they would contact to get a loan to buy a home someday. One girl raised her hand. "I am going to ask the government for that loan," she said. It became clear I was dealing with a classroom full of students who saw no future in pursuing entrepreneurship, had no confidence they would ever invest any money, and were not thinking about careers that could support a family someday. I was in the belly of pessimism. Although I am completely wide-eyed about the fact that my one class did not change their lives, I do realize that an ongoing campaign of financial literacy is needed to help people think strategically about their financial decisions. Poor families in the inner cities are not the only people who can be financially illiterate. I have seen doctors, lawyers, and small business owners (all smart people) behave in ways that demonstrate financial illiteracy. The multi-generational conse-quences of financial illiteracy are too significant to overlook.

My business partner, Mike Helgesen, and I have created a new experience for investors who need help in this area. The project is called "Dynamic Mapping." Dynamic Mapping is a financial planning method that is human-centered, rather than the normal spreadsheet output we might expect from traditional financial planning software. The output from Dynamic Mapping is graphed and creates a picture of a sailboat. The construction of the sailboat will depend on the inputs from the investor. If the boat is built well, it will have a very high prob-ability of reaching its destination. If it is not well built, the probability goes down dramatically. The boat metaphor is easily understood, inspires a visceral response from the investor, and encourages stra-tegic conversations with certified Dynamic Mapping advisors that are based on both parties having a clear understanding of the data.

Let's take a look at an example.

Amy and Joe

Amy and Joe are both 50 years of age and are beginning to plan for their retirement. They would like to retire at 65. They both have 401(k) plans into which they save steadily, along with some matching dollars from their employers. They refinanced their home five years ago. Their mortgage amortizes $200,000 over 30 years at 3.875% interest. The monthly payment is $940.47. Together, they contribute $800 per month into their 401(k) plans and their employers contrib-ute another $452 per month, so their total monthly contribution is $1,252. Amy and Joe assume their investments will earn 5% from a combination of interest, dividends, and principal appreciation.

Joe's sketch in figure 1-5 below advances their assets and liabilities from age 50 to their central organizing moment, their retirement at age 65. The current values of their retirement assets and mortgage are depicted at their present age, and both assets and liabilities proceed upward from there. The assets rise because they are growing from contributions and total return while the mortgage liability line climbs toward zero as Amy's and Joe's monthly mortgage payments reduce the outstanding balance.

Our task is to help them formulate a retirement plan. Don't worry about sourcing the numbers that make up the graph. The objective at this moment is to see how mapping reveals information which in turn, enables you to make better decisions. Figure 1-5 is my idea of revealing art.

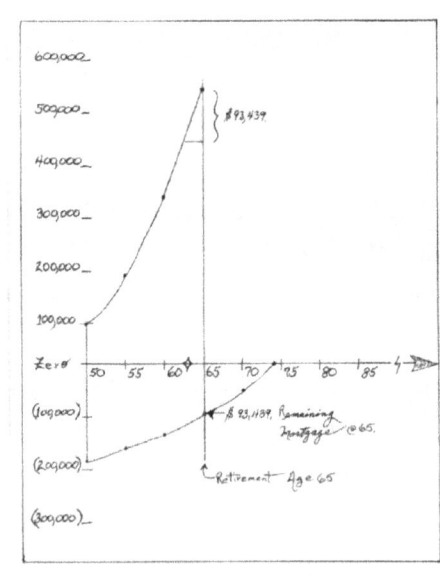

Figure 1-5: Time is the horizontal value and dollars are the vertical value. Assets are growing while debt is being paid down and the central organizing moment is retirement at age 65.

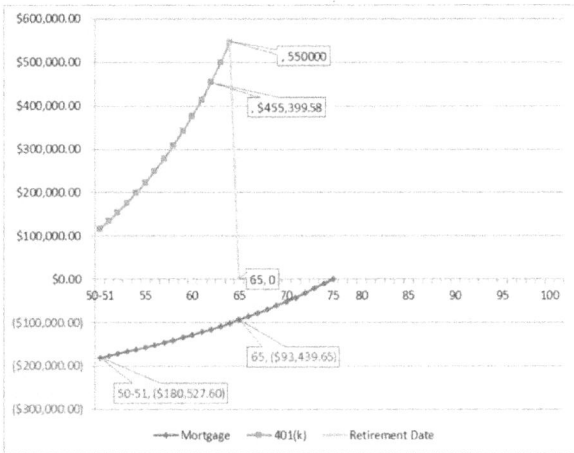

Figure 1-6: Here's Amy's Excel version of Joe's map.

Observations

First, observe Amy's and Joe's lifeline scudding across the center of Joe's map. It illustrates their current age at 50 years old and 15 years between their present age and their planned retirement age.

Next, observe their assets. Their current assets are shown on the dollar line at a value of $100,000. That value rises to about $546,000 over the next 15 years. This rise is caused by an assumed growth rate of 5% plus our couple's future contributions and their employer's match.

Finally, notice their liabilities. Recall that the $200,000 mortgage is a 30-year debt. Since five years have elapsed, it will continue for another 25 years and is mapped accordingly. After paying $940.47 per month for five years, the present balance is now -$180,527. That's the value shown on the map on the extreme left side at Joe's and Amy's present age. The liability line has an upward trajectory that will reach -$156,899 in five years as noted on the map and will continue to rise to -$93,439 at Joe's and Amy's retirement. It still has a balance of $51,225 at age 70, and finally attains zero in twenty-five years when Amy and Joe are 75 years old.

Analysis

Remember that the theme of this chapter is that most people lack a central or organizing idea about their financial situation, and even quality data won't render a solution without a process to channel it. Here's the process.

Look at Amy's and Joe's map. Does it stimulate a conversation about their debt in preparation for retirement? What jumps off the page? Yes! Their debt is carried 10 years into their retirement. Those years may be the healthiest and most active ones of their post-retirement lives, the ones they'll want to spend enjoying their newfound freedom.

Why would Joe and Amy have planned to have a post-retirement mortgage? Well, you know why, don't you? They probably believed as many people do, that they would be paying off the end of their mortgage with inflation-cheapened dollars and that their mortgage is an income tax deduction. Since they refinanced for 30 years, we can reasonably assume that either their monthly cost was lowered or they pulled out some cash. They may have had tuition bills to pay and needed some relief, or they may have consolidated some expensive debt accumulated during the financial tumults of life and the expense of raising their family.

Let's not speculate on the past but instead analyze the facts as they present themselves today. Joe and Amy may indeed pay the last few years of their mortgage with inflation-cheapened dollars, but as their advisor, I would ask them to reconsider that notion. Nearly all the retirees I have interviewed over the years hold each dollar dearly and would be more comfortable being debt-free.

As to their mortgage being a deduction, that's a bit erroneous. They will not receive a substantial tax deduction. Banks receive the bulk of the total interest paid to them during the first half of a mortgage's term. By the time Amy and Joe reach age 65, they will have already paid most of the interest. They may or may not know that only the interest portion of their mortgage payments is deductible and that the principal portion is not deductible. Also, if they find themselves in a lower tax bracket after they retire, the deduction they receive will be less valuable. Finally, although it may be transitory, under current tax law, many people will not file a schedule A and will instead take the standard deduction. That renders the tax augment disputable for many people.

Finally, Amy and Joe may have to take distributions from their retirement assets in order to meet the monthly mortgage obligation. That would be too bad because they would be removing money at least five years before withdrawals are required by the government, which will be in the year they become 70.5 years of age. This means they will be paying taxes on the withdrawals from their retirement plan in order to pay for a mortgage that carries either no deduction or a paltry and ever-reducing one. This is a plan that needs attention.

Solution

The map indicates that the remaining balance of our couple's mortgage will be $93,439 when they retire. A quick call to the lender or review of the DM APP will reveal that by adding $384 per month now, Amy and Joe will be mortgage-free by age 65. By doing so, they'll save over $40,000 dollars in interest, and have an additional $11,285.64 to spend in Venice, Italy or some other dream location of their choosing each and every year of the first ten years of their retirement. Hmmm, Venice dream vacations or bank payments and afternoons at the town's pool? Let's set our client's course for Venice, shall we?

Planning details regarding Amy & Joe:

Amy and Joe receive additional planning benefits when they prepay their mortgage. If our couple was forced into early retirement, then having a smaller principal would be useful as follows:

- They could stop prepaying and return to the lower, original monthly payment.
- They could sell their home and realize more equity.
- They could refinance the reduced principal in order to reduce their outflow. [This action is contingent on rates being good and their qualification on one salary].

Other Planning notes:

Some people may suggest the additional $384 could be invested instead of prepaying the mortgage. In this way, Joe and Amy might earn a higher return than the 3.875% mortgage interest rate. I agree the suggestion has merit, but I've noticed over the years that most people making suggestions like that don't have clients, they have a column or a blog. Their advice rarely accounts for the vagaries of the market, personal taste for risk, human behavior, or capital gain taxes.

However, if you choose to garner this opportunity for greater returns, then I suggest you set up a discreet fund in which to invest the $384 per month. When the value of the account approximates the remaining mortgage principal including the cost of capital gain taxes, you may liquidate the account, pay the taxes, and attend their mortgage burning party. The nice advantage to such a sinking fund is that it would also serve clients as a source of liquid capital readily available for opportunities or in an emergency.

Hint: You would be well-advised to reduce the risk characteristics of their mortgage cancellation fund as the time shortens or, better yet, take periodic gains and use the gains to hammer down the mortgage principal; these actions will prevent years of saving from being reversed during an economic downturn. Absent a little smart planning, such an event will leave your client with meager savings and stuck in the original mortgage.

There's More!

Observe the 401(k)s increase during the years approaching their retirement date. Do you notice anything interesting?

You're correct if you noticed that the 401(k)s are projected to increase by $93,439 during the last few years leading up to their retirement. I notated the moment on the sail when the 401(k)s were about $93,439 smaller than their ultimate value. That moment occurs about 2.5 years prior to retirement.

Does the fact that the last 2.5 years of savings and growth in their 401(k)s match the value of their mortgage at age 65 induce a topic worth mentioning to Amy and Joe? It should inspire you to open an early retirement conversation around the following question: Is it possible for Amy and Joe to retire early if they prepay enough principal to pay off their mortgage early?

The answer is that it is certainly possible. Although there are many factors which determine the timing of retirement, one important metric is the relationship of income to expenses. Removing an $11,285.64 mortgage expense from their annual budget, as well as the extra monthly principal payment required to prepay it, reduces their post-retirement expenses and opens the door for an early retirement conversation. It's unlikely that this action alone would lead to a two-year earlier retirement because the addition of two additional retirement years without the benefit of Social Security income would counterweigh some of the benefit, but it's an idea worth exploring. Our probing questions might lead them to a different discussion. Perhaps one of them could retire sooner or even swap careers for one that he or she had been dreaming about but didn't dare consider because the alternate career didn't have as large a compensation package as their existing job. Making such a career move might even enable one of them to continue working a few years beyond age 65 because he or she would be more fulfilled. Additionally, they could still consider retiring sooner, just not two years sooner.

This is the kind of experience people can expect from Dynamic Mapping-certified advisors. Our focus is on preserving wealth in multiple ways (from the pain of bear markets, excessive taxation, and the devastating impact of frivolous and/or fraudulent lawsuits), restoring the family's time to focus on the important relationships in life, and maintaining a high degree of privacy and discretion.

A free, downloadable app is available on the iOS and Android app stores to help manage the mathematical challenges of Dynamic Mapping. Feel free to use it yourself or share with a DM-certified advisor to open an important dialogue supporting your financial literacy!

CHAPTER 7

THE IMPORTANT ROLE OF INSURANCE IN REAL ESTATE

By **JOSH WHISLER**

A few days after a natural disaster, I received a call from a frantic property owner whose investment property was devastated by a major hurricane. After empathizing with the owner, I asked her to send me the insurance documentation as soon as possible. After reviewing the policy, I was disturbed but not surprised at what I read. Unfortunately, I had to inform the owner that the insurance policy she had for her investment was not worth the paper it was written on. The policy of insurance, issued by a large carrier, excluded hurricane damage and even if it had covered this peril, her maximum coverage for property damage was limited to $10,000.

Too many times I have seen honest, hardworking property owners pay their insurance premiums thinking they were fully covered for life's hurdles, only to discover their 60-page policy didn't cover or left them underinsured for the basic risks which they eventually suffer.

From properties that are an arm's-length from the shore without flood policies, properties in earthquake or landslide-prone areas without Difference in Conditions coverage to investment rental properties mistakenly issued homeowner policies, the cost of rebuilding often proves too high to recover after a loss, but all can be prevented with the proper selection of policy and coverages.

Don't wait until it's too late. Just because someone is licensed to sell you insurance does not mean they are truly qualified or have your best interests at heart. Make sure you review your policy annually and don't choose insurance based on the price of the premiums; select a policy that will have you covered when a loss or disaster occurs. In today's environment, it is not a question of if a disaster will strike but rather a question of when.

When purchasing real estate, insurance often becomes nothing more than a secondary thought. In the hustle of locating properties and negotiating terms, insurance is seen as a necessary evil that only slows down the purchasing process. Even the National Association of Realtors downplays the role insurance has in real estate transactions, only recommending that the search for coverage begins no later than when the contract is signed (the closing date).

But waiting so long into the purchasing process may have significant undesirable consequences. Buyers may learn premiums are unaffordable, coverage options are limited, or the property is simply uninsurable. Any such scenario could quickly derail the promise of a completed sales transaction.

Astute real estate agents and investors, however, understand the importance of having the ability to obtain the right insurance at an expected and manageable premium. Knowing ahead of time the impact insurance will contribute to the bottom line affords more leverage in a real estate deal. Better than expected insurance affordability can increase a property's attractiveness, while higher premiums or limited coverage options can have the opposite effect.

To provide additional comfort to your clients as an agent, or uncover new opportunities as an investor, having more than a cursory understanding of insurance is akin to adding a sharpened arrow to your quiver. Although insurance is a very broad and complex product, you must become familiar with common terms and coverages. As your insurance knowledge increases, add insurance-related questions to your discovery process to broaden your value and avoid potential pitfalls.

Most insurance policies use either a basic, broad, or special perils form. What perils (specific cause of damage) are covered within the owner's policy can greatly impact their coverage. Let's examine the differences between each policy form:

Basic peril forms include coverage for:
- Fire
- Lightning
- Windstorm or hail
- Explosion
- Smoke
- Vandalism
- Aircraft or vehicle collision
- Riot or civil commotion
- Sinkhole collapse
- Volcanic activity

Although the above list may seem comprehensive, consider the additional perils covered on the broad form:
- Burglary and break-in damage
- Falling objects
- Weight of ice and snow

- Freezing of plumbing
- Accidental water damage
- Artificially generated electricity

Both the basic and broad forms are specified peril policy forms. Or in other words, only the perils specifically stated are covered under the policy. For most comprehensive policy types, agents and investors should be looking for a special peril form policy, also known as an "all-risk policy."

Instead of listing what is covered, the special perils policy form covers all exposures except for those specifically excluded. Generally stated, unless there is an exclusion listed on the policy, coverage will be afforded.

The difference between basic, broad, and special form policies is one reason why policy premiums can vary so greatly. When evaluating the carrying costs for a property, be sure to understand how much coverage is being provided if you use the current owner's policy information. And even then, have the policy reviewed by an insurance professional to identify any unsavory exclusions or policy language.

Exclusions and Insurability

The insurance industry is a $1.2 trillion behemoth with property and casualty insurance, accounting for just less than half of every premium dollar. Many policyholders forget that at the end of the day, the insurance companies are businesses that care about their bottom line and what their earning numbers will be at the end of the quarter. Since insurance companies are made to run as profitable businesses, the less money flowing out in terms of benefits provides a higher profit for carriers. This is one reason when reviewing a policy, only a small percentage of the language in the policy is dedicated to what's covered and the rest is legalese intended to carve out several exceptions that exclude coverage. Neither the Insurance Services Office (ISO) or your local state agency governing insurance writes insurance policies; insurance company attorneys do. As such, most insurance policies are riddled with exclusions and exceptions. And when a property may be insurable today, changes in circumstances may make the structure uninsurable tomorrow.

Some exclusions may seem obvious and acceptable, such as war, neglect, nuclear hazard, and intentional act exclusions. However, for most property owners in the country, at least one or more perils are routinely excluded from their insurance policy due to their location.

The most common, location-specific exclusions exclude damage caused by:
- Wildfires
- Sinkholes
- Earthquakes
- Hurricanes (or named storm)
- Floods (regardless of location)

Coverage for excluded perils may be added back by endorsement or provided under a separate, stand-alone policy. Determining the cost of insurance for any home or structure needs to include the additional premium required to provide full coverage.

For the most part, insurance markets exist to fill in coverage gaps standard insurance companies typically exclude. However, there are special circumstances that could make a building partially or completely uninsurable.

For example, central Florida has been ravished by sinkholes. A statewide database has been developed by the insurance industry which, if a property appears within it, the property will be denied the ability to obtain any coverage for sinkhole. Similarly, the National Flood Insurance Program (NFIP) will also limit or reject coverage for properties having suffered multiple flood insurance claims. The insurability of a property should be learned much sooner than the closing date.

Flood Insurance

Flooding occurs in all 50 states and is the most common natural disaster in the United States. Dams or levees breaking, storms, wind, and snowmelt all can cause flooding. So, too, can new development, by changing the way water flows above and below ground. As little as one inch of flooding can cost more than $25,000 in damage.

Insurance coverage for flooding is typically **excluded** from homeowners and commercial property policies. Most flood insurance is provided separately through the National Flood Insurance Program (NFIP), although more private insurers are entering the marketplace.

Flood insurance abides by several complicated rules, making it imperative coverage requirements are examined long before the closing date. Federally backed mortgages require property owners to purchase flood insurance if the structure is in what is called a Special Flood Hazard Area (SFHA).

Do not rely on the property owner or their agent to advise you in which zone a property is located. Flood hazard maps can and do change. Your local insurance agent or a visit to FEMA's website can help you determine if a risk is situated in an SFHA.

If there is a flood insurance policy currently in place, however, make sure to ask for a copy. In some circumstances when the flood zone has changed from low to high hazard, the purchaser may be able to transfer the current owner's policy over to themselves. This will allow the new owner to retain the lower rates enjoyed under the current policy. If a policy is not transferred prior to closing, a new policy will be subject to the latest flood zone information, possibly at a much higher premium.

Even if a property is not in an SFHA, it does not mean there isn't a risk of flooding. More than 30% of all flood claims happen **outside** of special flood hazard areas. Take the time to ask neighboring property owners and community officials about any experiences they have had with flooding near the property being considered.

Valuation Methods

Every property insurance policy specifies how the amount of claim payment will be determined. The most favorable method for the property owner is on a replacement cost basis. Claims made under replacement cost language mean the insurance company will reimburse the full cost of replacing property.

Less favorable to the insured, but standardized by insurance companies, is the use of actual cash value. Most courts define actual cash value as the cost to replace the property with new but of like kind and quality, minus depreciation. This represents the dollar amount you could reasonably expect to receive if you were to sell an item or piece or property "as is."

When considering the purchase of a piece of property, knowing which valuation method is available from the insurance market will determine if additional reserve funding may be required. For example, a 25-year-old home or building may only receive its actual cash value in the event of a fire. This means the buyer will have to consider the additional expense it will take to repair or replace damaged property.

The availability of replacement cost for insurance purposes is often geographically determined. Roof age in areas prone to hurricanes will see more insurance policies impose actual cash value until such time the roof is updated to the newest codes. Insurers of properties in earthquake zones prefer new or retrofitted structures before offering replacement cost valuation.

Regardless of your location, an insurance company may not offer a replacement cost valuation for a variety of reasons. Learn beforehand the valuation methods available on a property before a purchasing decision is made.

Tenants and Occupancies

Dwellings, multi-family buildings, and condominiums all share similar exposures when it comes to occupancy. While rented units often have slightly higher risks associated with them as compared to owner-occupied residences, an insurance underwriter's primary concern with residential property is its vacancy rate.

Residential structures that are vacant or have high vacancy rates may have more difficulty obtaining property insurance than those considered fully rented. Furthermore, insurance policies very often will reduce coverage if a property has been vacant for a specified duration of time, typically 30 to 90 days.

Commercial properties, on the other hand, pose more of an issue for underwriters of both property and liability insurance. Before making an offer, review with your insurance agent the tenants expected to be in place after a purchase. The occupants of a building will have a direct impact on a structure's insurability and premium.

For property coverage, insurers will examine if any occupants increase fire or water hazards. For example, properties with a restaurant using open flame cooking will have higher property insurance rates than if an accountant occupied the same space. From a liability perspective, the amount of foot traffic is carefully considered. The higher the volume, the higher the risk for a slip and fall claim.

Liability Insurance

Whether the next purchase is a home, apartment building complex, or a commercial warehouse, all property owners have liability exposure. Liability insurance policies protect individuals and businesses from the risk they have from being held liable and sued for injury or negligence.

Liability insurance for property owners falls into three basic categories:
- General liability
- Bodily injury liability
- Property damage liability

General liability insurance protects insureds from a variety of claims and the costs related to them, including out-of-court settlements, litigation fees, and court judgments. Bodily injury liability specifically helps pay the costs of people injured or killed in an accident. Lastly, property damage liability helps pay for other people's property damaged in an accident (not the insured's property).

Homeowners need to be made aware of any exposures that may increase their policy premiums or result in an exclusion. Common exposures to identify include swimming pools, trampolines, and attractive nuisances, such as fountains or playgrounds.

For multi-family or commercial property buyers, the liability exposure increases, as the public will likely be visiting your property. In addition, there are typically more physical exposures present, such as power lines, fencing, drainage, and on-site equipment. There are very few laws governing the liability insurance requirements for commercial properties. Therefore, it is recommended to obtain a comprehensive risk management survey to identify exposures and use it to obtain a pre-purchase liability insurance quote.

Summary

Insurance plays a critical role in the purchase and ownership of real estate. Having a basic understanding of exposures associated with a property helps in selecting great properties over regular ones. But how insurance works to protect that property from those exposures is what sets great real estate agents and investors apart from the average Joe.

When the next potential property purchase appears on the horizon, follow these three tips for a smooth insurance transaction:

1. Talk to your trusted insurance professional before placing an offer.
2. Shop for the right insurance coverage, not the cheapest.

3. Follow up every conversation with an email to create documentation.

The best approach when purchasing real estate is to include your trusted insurance agent and your property insurance attorney as a part of your team. Their expertise can add tremendous value by identifying potential risk exposures, consulting on your coverage options, and procuring coverage exactly when you need it. Finally, after you have purchased your coverage make sure to review your policy annually for any changes, updates, and gaps.

CHAPTER 8

WHY USING A PRIVATE LENDER FOR BRIDGE LOANS IS BENEFICIAL

By **MARK ATALLA**

I was very young when I started in the banking industry. At just 18, I started as a bank teller at Wells Fargo, before learning about the lending business. I worked for a couple of smaller companies before starting my own business in 2009.

Over the decade that followed, I've successfully built Carlyle Capital into a thriving private lending and asset management company helping real estate investors acquire, refinance, restructure, and develop real estate holdings. Carlyle Capital is now one of the top Southern California private lending firms with the ability to successfully fund multi-million dollar transactions all the time and help investors in a way big banking just can't.

Carlyle Capital's primary lending programs focus on providing short-term bridge financing secured by residential, multifamily, and commercial real estate.

Private Lenders vs. Banks

I get this question all the time and it is very important that investors know the difference between private lending, hard money lending, and bank lending. If you aren't sure which one you're working with, ask. Lenders will happily disclose the information.

Private lenders are regular people or groups of people who are not banks and can offer to loan you money on their own terms at their discretion. Carlyle Capital is essentially a private bank, meaning there is discretionary capital, controlled by an investment committee on behalf of individuals who have entrusted Carlyle Capital to diversify and mitigate the risk of their cash by following a disciplined investment strategy. Since the deals are ultimately funded by people and not government-backed institutions, the funding guidelines are specific and focus primarily on the asset itself and its value, and less on the real estate investor's tax returns.

Since private lenders do not rely on banks or the government, guidelines are more flexible than with institutional banks. Private lending is often the best option for real estate investors and developers, as it typically allows them the ability to acquire real estate that a bank would ordinarily not approve them for and provides leverage points that are attractive. It is also more cost-effective than having to find a partner who can contribute more cash to the deal, which would allow a bank to finance it but a private lender would still be able to fund independently. Since your individual credit score is only one factor and the loan terms are often negotiable, private lenders are ready to help facilitate your next real estate investment.

The disciplined guidelines of private money lenders are primarily based on two things: the asset and the borrower's ability to successfully complete their investment objective to pay the money back on the loan. Private money lenders will often offer loans to those who have been rejected by banks.

Hard money lending is where private lending began. That is, hard money loans are secured by the "hard asset" of real estate but with even looser guidelines than today's private lenders. Hard money lenders will fund transactions that even some private lenders may not touch, including foreclosure bailout loans. This typically would come at a much higher cost, and perhaps lower leverage. These loans can also be funded by private sources, but quite often can be looked at as the lender of last resort due to the higher costs they entail. However, sometimes they are the only options available for a real estate investor who has gotten themselves in a tough place.

Lastly, we all know that big banks will scrutinize everything about the borrower and the deal before funding: full credit underwriting, full income documentation, full expense analysis, debt to income calculations, total loans outstanding, and more. Their loans tend to be non-negotiable and have very specific terms, making them more of a take it or leave it type of loan option. These are also the organizations most likely to say no to real estate investors who don't have an 800+ credit score and exceptionally strong verifiable income to afford to pay their mortgage payments for 30 years. They quite often ignore the fact that a real estate investor's business plan may only be a short-term investment or may involve leasing a property so it pays for itself.

When I founded Carlyle Capital, I raised funds from family investment offices and private investors who saw the potential of this previously untapped market. I started with some smaller projects, such as gas station deals, and once people saw what we were doing and how beneficial bridge loans from private lenders were, suddenly people were approaching me left and right to get money for their real estate projects. As the big banks were saying no, we could say yes.

What is a bridge loan?

For real estate investors, bridge loans are extremely important to understand.

A bridge loan is a temporary loan that allows the borrower to meet their real estate investing objectives and is meant to be paid off in 12-36 months by either selling the property or refinancing with a longer-term loan.

As most successful real estate investors don't report strong enough W2 income to qualify for bank financing, bridge loans focus primarily on the assets as collateral. That is the property itself and the borrower's ability to contribute cash to close a transaction. This allows real estate investors the potential for acquiring and flipping properties in a scalable way. This short-term loan essentially "bridges the gap" to help a real estate investor make an investment when traditional banks would not be able to squeeze them into their rigid guidelines.

For investors who are looking to purchase or refinance a non-owner-occupied residential property, a bridge loan can provide access to quick capital, and it relies on the value of the collateral more than the strength of the ability for the borrower to repay the loan.

As the loan typically has a short life span, interest-only payments (rather than being amortized) can potentially be included as part of the loan amount (in cases of refinancing with sufficient equity) to prevent the need for any monthly payments. Whether the bridge loan is being used to purchase a property, refinancing to purchase other real estate properties, expanding a business, restructuring debt, buyout partners, divorce, or any other non-real estate venture, a bridge loan is an opportunity to get expeditious capital to meet your needs.

7 Benefits of Using a Private Lender for Real Estate Investments

Access to capital, especially short-term capital like bridge loans, is a critical aspect of real estate investing and many experienced real estate professionals prefer private lenders over more traditional mortgage or loan providers.

As an experienced private lender, I can give you a million reasons why you should consider using a private lender for your next real estate investment deal, but here are seven specific ones. I have seen these benefits personally work for hundreds of deals and even survived through the recession when banks were scrambling and not lending money to those who needed it. Private lenders have the flexibility to take on projects institutionalized banks won't and take more risks.

Benefit #1: Customized Lending Services

Unlike big banks, private lenders don't have to use the "established" frameworks for lending money. We operate on a case-by-case basis and can customize the deal to fit the investors' and borrowers' needs and timeline. Instead of being rejected by a bank because you don't fit their rigid criteria, we have the ability to lend money based on your assets and not your personal credit history, which further allows us to tailor to your needs.

Benefit #2: Flexible Requirements

As a private lender, we can choose to ignore less-than-perfect credit history. After the recession, banks have tightened up their lending requirements, leading to more loan rejections. Private lenders have much more flexible credit requirements, as our lending is based more on the asset than the individual.

The same holds true for income requirements and other factors traditional lenders scrutinize. Private lenders are able to analyze many factors and choose to loan money to those who need it at our own discretion, instead of having to adhere to predetermined criteria.

Benefit #3: Faster Approval Times

The real estate market changes every day and waiting too long to secure a loan can screw up deals for real estate professionals. Many investors are looking for a faster "yes" and having the money in their pockets to be able to successfully negotiate their deals. Private lenders are able to accelerate the loan approval and expedite the entire underwriting process. Due to flexible teams and support, private lenders respond to clients quickly and don't need to spend weeks considering and confirming mortgage approval.

Benefit #4: Flexible Loan Terms

Institution banks often require longer loan terms, whereas private lenders can do shorter-term deals faster. Because we are privately owned and not regulated in the same way as banks, private lenders also have the ability to negotiate loan terms so that all parties are happy with the terms. We are also able to make faster decisions on your negotiations and meet with you personally to discuss them.

Benefit #5: No Penalty for Prepayment

Many banks will impose fees and penalties for prepaying your loans back to them. But because private lenders are using their own money to invest, the borrower has more control over their loans and the lenders are often happy to receive prepayment.

Benefit #6: Competitive Interest Rates

Money lending is a competitive industry, and since we are specifically lending money in the real estate market, private lenders understand that market very well. We are able to offer competitive interest rates on short-term loans and get the borrower paid as soon as they need it to complete their deal.

Benefit #7: Local Market Expertise

This one is a huge benefit to real estate investors and professionals. Unlike banking giants like Bank of America and HSBC, private lenders are local market players. We excel in not just identifying local investment opportunities, we use local experts and resources to evaluate deals and know the local realtors and investors. We can partner with people we actually know and understand their track record to find unconventional deals for our investors, limit potential pitfalls, and close deals faster.

Summary

Building my own successful private lending firm at the height of the recession was not easy, nor is it always easy now. But I love every minute of what I do, including mentoring others, teaching people about the business, and giving back to my community. I have worked every day to outwork and outsmart my competition, from being the consistently top sales earner in my first-ever mortgage job at 21 to now building a sustainable company helping others achieve their goals. As a first-generation U.S. citizen, I have been able to realize my American dream while having the pleasure of helping others achieve theirs.

If you are a real estate investor or realtor looking to secure financing on your first, fifth, or fiftieth project, you'll find the benefits of using a private lender far outweigh the name of big institutionalized banks. I'd love to talk to you further about how private loans will benefit you and your business and help you grow at a faster rate than you thought possible.

CHAPTER 9

CREATING A PATH TO FINANCIAL FREEDOM

By **RYAN COTTER**

We all know that owning real estate is one of the best ways to generate passive income, but how does one get started? The points of entry seem endless. Do you want to start with a single-family condo or buy a vacation rental property or invest in a large 100-unit apartment building?

The possibilities begin to feel so overwhelming that the majority of potential first-time investors talk themselves out of the process before they get started. By doing so, they continue to throw away large sums of money every month to their largest liability - a housing payment. For the average American, a monthly mortgage is their largest financial liability following them throughout their lives, but it does not have to be. I work with clients to eliminate this liability by teaching them how to understand the rules of real estate and, more importantly, real estate lending in order to create a path to financial freedom.

The rules are not complicated, but because most people do not know this they never step up to the plate. Once potential buyers understand the basics, they can play the game of real estate effectively. I help educate my clients on the rules of the game so they can understand how the real estate and real estate lending games work.

During my twenty years in the real estate and finance world amassing a real estate empire, I have learned one of the most important rules of real estate is to buy an income-producing property before you buy anything else. I can not stress enough how important it is that your first piece of property is an income-producing property with a low-down-payment program.

One common misconception buyers have is that they must first buy a condo or single-housing unit before an investment property. It seems to make sense that you would start small as you build your real estate portfolio, but this is a mistake. Once a single-family property is purchased, the buyer loses the chance to purchase a multi-unit property with a low down payment, making the barrier for purchasing an investment property too high for your average investor.

I specialize in two-to-four unit multi-family income-producing properties with low-down-payment options. I recommend to my clients that they start their investment portfolios with the purchase of a fourplex. A four-unit building is the largest building you can buy with a Federal Housing Administration loan, which guarantees a low down payment and a 30-year fixed loan.

I bought a fourplex one year after graduating from college. I fixed it up and then rented three of the units out to friends. That single purchase served as my springboard to financial wealth and freedom.

If you really want to get into real estate development, own properties, and have financial freedom, I recommend jumping into the deep end. Buy a fourplex and get your hands dirty. If you love it after a year, then you can move onto buying your next piece of property. If it is not for you, then it is better to learn it right away.

By buying a fourplex unit, moving into one of the units, then renting the other three you go from being a rent-paying tenant to a rent-*producing* tenant (and landlord) in a matter of weeks.

Let's say your rent is $1500 a month. You decide to buy a fourplex. You live in one of the units while renting the other three units. The money you generate from the three units will cover the mortgage, saving you $1500 a month. I tell clients not to treat that $1,500 a month as extra spending money, but to save it to put toward a down payment for their next property. After a year, that $1,500 per month accumulates into $18,000, which is a great down payment for the next piece of property.

The steps are simple. Buy a fourplex, live rent-free with a cash positive of $1,500 a month, then over time, vacate that fourth unit and buy another piece of property. At that point, you will have another $1,500 more per month you can put toward the mortgage of the new property. If you buy another property, you do it again the next year and you save that money, too. Not only will you be making the $1,500 a month from the unit you are living in, but you will also be saving $1,500 a month by not having an obligation, so over the course of the next 12 months, you will save $36,000 - again, for the down payment of the next place.

After purchasing and living in a fourplex for a year, I encourage clients to buy a triplex, then a duplex, then a single-family home. I give clients a realistic plan to acquire nine units that will pay their complete housing costs. *Once the mortgage is paid off, the property becomes a cash positive asset.* Additionally, you are getting great tax write-offs while you are doing this. As the cherry on top, there is appreciation over the next 20 or 30 years on this property.

Buyers who follow the conventional wisdom of buying a single-family home before an investment property lose the low down payment option. If you buy the single-family home first before buying a fourplex, you will have to put down 20-25 percent down on the fourplex. That type of money makes the purchase unattainable for most buyers.

The fixed mortgage is another rule of the game. The cheap 30-year fixed mortgage rate maxes out on fourplex properties. You can't buy a five-unit property and get a 30-year fixed mortgage. That fixed rate is the safety mechanism that saves you money over time. The beauty of this system is that you acquire a building with a 30-year fixed mortgage and then you let your tenants pay the asset off over time. Over time as you raise rents, it will allow you to accelerate that debt elimination. As your tenant's rents increase year-to-year, your mortgage stays the same, allowing you to pay it off in less than 30 years.

Another rule of the real estate game that supports this line of action is underwriting. *A lender looks at buyers of a duplex, triplex, or fourplex in the exact same light as buyers of a single-family house.* This means the qualification standards and down payment requirements are much more attainable, especially for first-time or younger buyers than larger real estate purchases. Larger investment properties require a much larger down payment, which takes most people out of the game. A buyer of a fourplex, however, can use a loan requiring as *little* as two percent down payment.

The key is that you have to live on the property. You are getting that small down payment because the banks see it as an "owner-occupied" property. It has to be your primary residence and the underwriter has to believe you will live there, otherwise, you have to put 20-25 percent down. If you already own a single-family home or condo and tell the bank you want to move from that to a fourplex, they are not going to believe you. People do not move in that direction. They move from fourplex to single-family homes, not single-family homes to a four-plex. If you start with the fourplex, I show people how you can put as little as two percent down and even get money to do renovations to the property on top of that. If you start with a single-family home and then go to a fourplex, you will be required to put as much as 25 percent down, which takes you out of the game.

The by-product of buying a 30-year fixed multi-unit property is generational wealth you can pass on to your children and grandchildren. I have heard many stories of someone passing on a building to one of their children and it has set them up for life. That building has paid for their college, paid for their wedding, and helped them buy their first house. On a 30-year fixed mortgage, the payment will not increase other than taxes for the next 30 years. If rent increases *over 30 years to combat inflation, such as the typical 3 to 5 percent, you will pay off that property in about 20 years.* So it will be cash positive or a cash cow from year 20 onward. Property values go in cycles but continuously goes up over time. The property will have all the equity so when you sell it, it will be worth a ton of money.

In any market, I would find an up-and-coming area that can give you an opportunity of value and the opportunity of a low-interest rate. In the future, prices will go down and rates will go up, giving you an opportunity to buy. You might be making base hits for a while, but that is where you will get the home run. When the market shifts again and rates go down and market value goes up, then you will have an opportunity to retrade the balance of that mortgage to a lower interest rate and can pay off the mortgage sooner.

Depending on your risk level, you could buy a four-unit, then a three-unit, then two-unit, then a single home property. Or you can go from a four-flat to a single home if after your first investment you realize you do not want to deal with it anymore.

This is not a get-rich-quick scheme or a no-money-down trick. This is for an approach to enhance and better your life over time. There is no better way of putting yourself on a path to financial freedom, but it takes patience. If you have that patience, buying income-producing properties is the number one way to get out of the rat race, build generational wealth for your children, and use other people's money to build wealth for yourself.

CHAPTER 10

ASSET PROTECTION FOR REAL ESTATE

By **S. BLAKE HARRIS**

Real estate investors know that rental properties can produce tremendous returns, but very few consider that real estate can also result in great risks for investors. I am not referring to a potential market downturn or the occasional difficult tenant, but rather to a lawsuit that could result in bankruptcy. In this chapter, I will discuss several different legal options investors can use to protect their rental properties. Whether it is a single-family home or an apartment building, commercial, residential, or undeveloped land, no real estate investor can afford to put their entire net worth at risk.

Why You Need to Protect Real Estate

Imagine for a moment that, after all your years of hard work, a tenant in one of your rental properties files a claim against you. Perhaps the tenant claims there's toxic mold in the home or undisclosed lead-based paint. Maybe it's not even one of your tenants – guests, workers, neighbors, even a trespasser who tripped over a downed tree limb on your property - have the right to sue you. The reality is a lawsuit can come anytime, even from the most unexpected sources. If you haven't taken any steps to protect yourself, you could lose your investments in order to satisfy a judgment against you.

Asset protection planning aims to reduce the potential liability from a future lawsuit. Protecting your property means developing a strategy that shields what you own from creditors. You do not need a multi-million dollar real estate portfolio to start thinking about asset protection, even a retiree trying to augment a pension with a single rental property needs to be aware of the potential legal risks.

The goal of asset protection is to use the laws available to protect what you own from creditors and to keep one bad turn of events from turning into a life-altering setback. Asset protection planning can keep you from losing your property – it's as simple as that. It's perfectly legal and can make a world of difference when negotiating a settlement agreement, but you must start the process well in advance. If you wait until someone is already suing you, it might be too late to properly protect against that particular claim.

There are several ways you can protect your real estate investments, including single-member LLCs, limited partnerships, and asset protection trusts. Most often, a combination of these will prove most effective in defending against a potential lawsuit.

Single-Member LLCs

Limited Liability Companies or LLCs are a type of legal business formation, and they are a popular and straightforward way to protect real estate holdings. When property is placed under an LLC, it can reduce the owner's personal exposure to risks surrounding that property, known as inside liability. When real estate is placed in an LLC, the property is treated as an autonomous business. It is considered a standalone business and is legally separate from its owner's other assets. If someone gets hurt on the property and sues, only the property which is under the LLC can be attached to pay a judgment, not the owner's personal property.

If you have more than one investment property, ideally you would create a separate LLC for each, so that a lawsuit related to one property would not potentially impact another. Let's say you own three properties (A, B, and C) and all three are under one LLC. If that trespasser was on property A when he tripped and fell, all three properties would be at risk to satisfy a judgment. But if each property is in its own LLC, only property A will have liability exposure.

The LLC represents an excellent way to shield you from inside liability, but what if there is a judgment against you related to your other business or professional activities, known as "outside liability"? Will the LLC protect your properties from that? The answer is that it depends on the law of the state where the claim is filed. In many states, a creditor cannot force you to turn over your membership interest in an LLC. Instead, those creditors' rights are limited to a charging order, which allows a creditor to take the debtor's share of any distributions from the business when those distributions are made.

As of right now, only five states provide charging order protection to single-member LLCs:

- Alaska
- South Dakota
- Nevada
- Delaware
- Wyoming

The remaining 45 states only provide charging order protection to multi-member LLCs and family limited partnerships.

Limited Partnership

A family limited partnership (FLP) is a holding company owned by two or more family members, created to protect a family's business interests, real estate, and other low-risk assets. One of the main benefits of using an FLP to hold real estate investments or other risky assets is that the FLP can be used to give you Charging Order Protection over your assets. This means that if a member of an FLP finds himself or herself in debt, the creditor cannot get access to the property inside the FLP or even to the debtor's share of the FLP in order to satisfy the debt. But, though this may sound favorable to creditors, it really isn't. If you find yourself in the debtor situation, a charging order gives you the ability to delay paying your creditors indefinitely by withholding distributions while paying yourself a salary to manage the FLP.

All states allow personal creditors of an FLP owner to get a charging order against the debtor-owner's FLP interest and in about two-thirds of states, the charging order is the creditor's only option. And, because the creditor is not allowed to order the FLP to make a distribution, creditors who obtain charging orders frequently end up with nothing. However, having that charging order against an FLP owner can make it difficult to take money out of an FLP business without having to pay the creditor first.

Another way that charging order protection can benefit you is that if the trespasser who sued you is successful and receives a charging order, it is likely that he will still be liable to pay taxes on the amount that you never pay him (as long as the FLP never makes a distribution). Letting the plaintiff's lawyer know upfront that you have a well-drafted FLP is a great way to deter a trespasser from suing in the first place! As many lawsuits are taken on a contingency basis, and an asset search will be one of the first things the attorney does before accepting a case, placing your assets into an FLP reduces the financial incentive for plaintiff's lawyers to come after you!

The original purpose of a charging order was not to protect the debtor's interest in the FLP, it was so that other members of the FLP would not have their interest endangered when one member found himself in hot water. This is different than a single-member LLC because there have been court opinions that have said if there are no other members in an LLC to protect, then the charging order protection should not exist.

Asset Protection Trust

Another way to protect your real estate investments is through an asset protection trust. Trusts are similar to corporations and LLCs in that they are considered separate legal entities. The trust must be "irrevocable" in order to be a separate legal entity. An irrevocable trust is a type of trust which terms typically cannot be modified, amended, or terminated without the approval of the named beneficiary or beneficiaries. Once the grantor transfers ownership of assets into the trust, he or she is no longer considered the legal owner of the assets inside the trust. As with an LLC or FLP, creditors can still attempt to get access to income from the trust, including most distributions.

In an asset protection trust, typically, you become the beneficiary of the trust, while someone else serves as the trustee. The trustee will hold the legal title, but you, as the beneficiary, will hold an equitable interest. This means that while the property held in trust is technically yours, you can't lose your assets due to a lawsuit. Usually what makes an asset protection trust different from another kind of trust is that it is a "self-settled" spendthrift trust. This means that you are both the settlor (the person who creates the trust) and the beneficiary (the person who gets to access the trust), but you may or may not be the trustee (the person who controls the trust), though you do maintain a certain amount of control over how the trust assets are used.

The spendthrift clause is a key provision of asset protection trusts because the trust is created for the benefit of someone who is not able to lose their assets to a judgment creditor or in a bankruptcy proceeding. By using the same language that was originally drafted to protect these so-called "spendthrift" beneficiaries into an asset protection trusts, we're able to protect assets from lawsuits. This is because the assets are under the control of the trustee rather than the settlor of the trust personally. This works because the trustee, rather than the settlor, is in charge. If a judge orders the settlor of the trust to turn over his assets to satisfy a judgment, the settlor can honestly state that it is the trustee, not himself, who has the authority to do so. Likewise, the trustee can state that he is legally obligated to follow the terms of the trust and maintain the assets until the lawsuit is resolved.

Conclusion

Asset protection in real estate protects you and your investments in case of a lawsuit or threat of legal action. Real estate investments are generally a significant source of wealth but also a significant source of risk. As such, they represent some of the most important assets to plan around, protect, and isolate from legal risks.

In this chapter, we have discussed several strategies for protecting your real estate holdings and determining what works best for you will vary depending on your circumstances and situation. If you would like to learn more about how to best protect your properties and yourself from the threat of a lawsuit, it is important to consult and work with a knowledgeable professional. Together with an asset protection attorney, you can create and execute a strategy that aligns with your goals and protects your real estate from the threat of lawsuits.

CHAPTER 11

PROPERTY MANAGEMENT: ALIGNING EXPECTATIONS WITH REALITY

By **SANTIAGO GROSSY**

Dear Board Member(s),

Yes! I'm speaking to you. Did you know that if the steps outlined in this chapter would have been followed, the complications that will be outlined in this chapter could have been avoided? This could have been circumvented by simply aligning your expectations with the reality of what it took to get such a task accomplished. As board members, we can sometimes be naïve, thinking that running a million-dollar company automatically qualifies you to participate on the board of a condominium or homeowners association. Truth be told, although your experience can bring valuable insight, it can also be a handicap. As Steve Jobs once said, "It doesn't make sense to hire smart people and then tell them what to do. We hire smart people so they can tell us what to do."

To fully understand the issues in this chapter, let's first identify the meaning of micromanaging. Micromanaging is when one controls the small details pertaining to a task or situation being performed by another. This has a negative effect in the workplace, as it reduces initiative and the willingness to perform. The obsession with controlling every detail leads to managerial failure. Micromanaging will certainly affect the output of others within your association. Resentment, lack of trust, lack of teamwork, malicious compliance, and hostile work environments can all be contributing factors to the failure of an organization.

One could argue that a board member has the best intentions when joining the board, and for the most part, they do. The problem is when the board or a board member considers themselves more versed on the subject of property management then the manager or the management entity they have hired. The paradox is that the board member, who originally joined the board to truly help move the community forward, is now the reason for its failure. This is exactly what happened with ABC Condominium Association, Inc.

In 2015, ABC Condominium had just held its election meeting and elected a new board member as President. The new board member had every intention to move the community forward and was extremely excited and eager to get started in his new role. The board member soon realized that things were not as easy as one might have thought. Projects fell behind and the operation started to deteriorate. The manager seemed unwilling to help and was stand-offish at times, and the board member did not understand why. He felt he was providing clear direction and support.

After continuous issues, the board gathered to discuss and approve the retention of a new management company, Affinity Management Services. The board felt that after an entire year, the community was ready for the change. Like any relationship, the first month was uneventful. The assigned manager was thankful for all the support being offered, although at times it was a bit overwhelming. The team did not know it then but soon realized that they were being micromanaged. They had no control over the operation, yet they were responsible for the outcome. The inability to implement their processes was affecting every opportunity for advancement. Every move was being monitored and the outcome was low morale and high stress. As the team brought forward solutions or mentioned success stories, the conversation was redirected to something that had not been accomplished. The pushback became apparent when attempting to implement analytical tools that would assist in determining peak times during office hours. The board simply said no. In addition, the board asked to be blind-copied on all emails and to have them listed as the only individuals able to speak to certain vendors.

Regardless of the circumstances, the team knew they had work to do, but how? The team was being blamed for cleaning, security, and even accounting. This made things more difficult, as cleaning, security, and accounting were all outsourced. Management had no authority to remove an employee, let alone make changes without board approval. When it came to accounting, the office team would handle all the calls and disputes, while the accounting firm balanced the books.

The board often neglected to remember that such issues were due to past failures and the goal was to correct those failures. The discussion went something like this:

Board:
- "I asked the manager to send this communication to the owners but I was surprised to hear that she had her assistant handle it when I gave it to her."
- "I told the manager a bottle was on the floor and 30 minutes later, it was still there."

- "I sat with the manager to dictate some letters to her and she stated that she could take care of this before the end of the day, as she was dealing with emergencies. Apparently, the boiler was not working. That only takes 30 minutes to resolve."
- "They are straightforward with responses. I don't feel like they want to do what they're told."
- "They like doing things on their own, but we like for a process to be in place before something is done so that the board can review it."

Management:

"I understand, but doesn't the board think that we may be throwing too much at the manager? We need to take into account the years of neglect and the number of projects being worked on at any given time. Not to take away from the comments provided, but may we analyze further?"

Unfortunately, the board did not see it that way. The management team did as one would expect: analyze the overall operation, including pending projects. It was apparent that the previous failures were due to the board's inability to take a step back and allow those they hired to perform. During the discovery stage, thousands of pages showed the board's unwillingness to let go, not allowing the manager to perform their job. This correlated to what was happening with the current team. This could also be attributed to overspending and incomplete projects.

It was clear that there was infighting amongst the board and a lack of trust, as three different engineers were hired for the same project, all overseeing one another. This drained the fund balance from one million dollars to under one hundred and fifty thousand dollars, with an incomplete project to show for it.

Dealing with micromanagers is difficult, as they tend to think they are always right. One must acknowledge the board and a plan of action should be drafted to address those concerns. Right or wrong, the plan must outline the steps that will be taken, even if the manager disagrees. Managers, you are the professional manager and you don't get paid to always agree, you are paid to provide guidance, even when it's against the board's wishes.

As a board member, do you believe that the actions above can lead to the success of the team who is representing you? A key symptom of being a micromanager is a lack of trust. How do we define trust? It is said that individuals who have trust issues tend to have unrealistic expectations, and they undeniably dislike letting go and giving up control to others. It was interesting to see how micromanagement and trust correlated with one another and the way it showed when discussing issues with the board.

Creating a Solution

Below are the steps Affinity Management Services felt would have the biggest impact while indirectly coaching the board on letting go. One must evaluate their progress to see what works for them. Consistency in executing the steps is crucial to truly gauge success.

Step #1:

The management team started communicating regularly and had the onsite team do the same. This was done by providing weekly reports, as well as daily updates on projects. The reports covered all the items the manager was working on while providing a visual on the workload being managed by the two team members.

Outcome: The board seemed more relaxed but their expectations were still the same. The reports provided the manager with some breathing room to be able to execute on other items, but board members still criticized things not getting done and neglected to review the reports being provided by the manager. Such reports showed how an office of two was handling over 20 projects, more than 15 emails (each) per day, and seven walk-ins, not including the number of calls, which they were unable to analyze because the board delayed the installation of the tracking system.

Step #2:

The management team started showing more empathy. They knew that the board's intentions were good and that their actions were not a reflection of who they were as people. Showing them that we cared allowed us to build trust.

Outcome: The board seemed more trusting at times and their demands for instant gratification diminished.

Step #3:

The management team started anticipating the needs of the board. This helped them stay ahead of the game. They recognized patterns and started anticipating certain needs.

Outcome: They were always ahead and the board felt that their vision was in line with their manager's vision. They continued to build trust.

In conclusion, when a board hires a management company, there needs to be sufficient trust to allow the hired professionals to perform their tasks. The board members and manager need to find a balance that outlines where the manager's duties begin and where the board's duties end. The board must remember that they are to provide the manager with direction, while the manager is the one who actually manages those directives. When the board is the director but also wants to manage, it imposes restraints on the operation, as the manager is not allowed to execute plans properly. They end up being managed by those who should be directing them.

Remember, the captain of the ship cannot also be the food and beverage director. Don't try to wear multiple hats - delegate and allow the manager to manage.

In the end, the management company continued enforcing the three steps listed above, which encouraged trust amongst everyone involved. This allowed the management company to manage the board's expectations and continue indirectly coaching the board daily. The steps taken alleviated the problem enough to allow the team to work. Unfortunately, it could not return the money that was lost from overspending due to a lack of trust and judgment. The manager was able to stop the bleeding and to move the project closer to completion but the board had an entirely new challenge: Explaining to the owners of the community how so much money was spent on projects that were never completed and what attributed to such failure.

What type of board member are you? For the purposes of higher learning, let's focus on the type of board member described above. You may have already been asking yourself this question.

Ask yourself these questions:

1. Do you feel that you need to review everything being done by the manager? Is there a constant battle between how the manager manages a project and how you want the project to be managed? (Y/N)
2. Do you ever catch yourself unhappy with the way things are being done by the manager? (Y/N)
3. Do you need to be notified of everything going on at the office, even when not directly pertaining to you? (Y/N)
4. Do you ask the manager to copy you on all emails or script their emails to your liking? (Y/N)
5. Do you want every little task to be documented and for a process to be established? (Y/N)
6. Do you feel as though you are smarter than the team you hired? (Y/N)
7. Do you consider yourself fixated on the day-to-day operations? (Y/N)
8. Do you give directives and then describe exactly how the task should be done? (Y/N)
9. Do you second-guess others when they are making decisions? (Y/N)
10. Do you need to know what the team is doing at all times? (Y/N)

The above survey is not an exact science but your answers should provide some clarity as to your way of thinking. Micromanagers tend to have high expectations, which makes it hard for others to live up to their standards. If you said yes to five or more, you are indeed a micromanager.

What are you going to do about it, now that you know what may happen as a result of over-managing and micromanaging?

CHAPTER 12

OPPORTUNITIES OUTSIDE CALIFORNIA

By **SEVAK KESHISHIAN**

As a lifelong Los Angeles resident, I know the benefits of living in this city. As a real estate broker who advises clients on what to do with their real estate investments, I have learned of the many benefits of purchasing investment properties outside of Los Angeles and, even more specifically, outside of California altogether.

One of the biggest benefits to owning and investing in multi-family properties is to build and create wealth. I am currently a Vice President of Investments with Marcus & Millichap, one of the nation's largest real estate firms. My team, The SK Group, specializes in helping our clients with purchasing and selling multifamily residential assets. These properties are bought and sold for millions of dollars.

Over the last 10 years, I have closed more than 120 transactions totaling almost half a billion dollars worth of real estate. I have lived in Los Angeles for more than 31 years and I love the area, but I have come to realize that investors can increase their cash flow by investing outside of Los Angeles and even more when investing outside of California. There are four main reasons for this.

Affordability

The old adage that a person should spend no more than 33 percent of their income on their living expenses has gone out the window. As housing prices and rents have increased, Los Angeles residents are spending roughly 50 percent of their income to cover their living expenses. This lack of affordability is causing renters and homeowners to seek lower costs of living, forcing them to move out of their neighborhoods in order to do so. The migration all over greater Los Angeles has never been more evident. The rapid rise and gentrification of neighborhoods in areas like West Adams, Jefferson Park, Atwater, Highland Park, Inglewood, and Leimert Park are proof that high rents and rising home prices force residents to seek a more affordable alternative.

As neighborhoods and communities gentrify, rents in the area increase. This increase is inevitably followed by an increase in property values. While this is good for existing owners of real estate and rental property, it typically means that investors who are seeking to purchase property in these neighborhoods have to pay higher prices and accept lower returns.

On the flip side, renters who are feeling the pinch of high housing costs are exploring options which include moving out of state where rents are more affordable. Californians are moving to states like Arizona, Texas, Oregon, and Colorado because of the lower cost of living. Over the last few years, many California-based companies have been exploring relocating their headquarters and leaving, too, because California taxes are so high. Companies are moving their headquarters or production sites to states like Arizona, Texas, and Nevada because of tax incentives and other less stringent regulations. The migration of residents spurs population growth in other states, making cities like Phoenix, Las Vegas, or San Antonio ripe for investment.

Cost of Ownership

Investors are seeing more bang for their buck. In other states, units cost less to maintain, cost less to turn over, and generally cost less per unit on average. One rental unit in Los Angeles is about three or four times more expensive than a unit in Texas. For example, a five-unit apartment building in Los Angeles can trade for $1,000,000 where that same building in Texas can trade for $350,000. The significant price difference is due to the rent for the same unit being much cheaper in Texas than in Los Angeles. The fact that it is cheaper to own and renovate units in states like Texas and Arizona provides a lot of flexibility for an investor to make a decent return on their property.

Easier Opportunities for Appreciation

Real estate appreciation in LA can be arbitrary, and now with AB 1482 being passed, a state bill that has implemented rent control for all rental properties built 15 years ago and older (i.e. built in or before 2005), repositioning rental properties with existing tenants has become harder than ever. In other states such as Arizona and Texas, there are no rent control laws, and this allows for investors to find rental properties which have been mismanaged and/or have significantly lower than market rents for an opportunity to reposition the property and appreciate its value through "sweat" equity. We define sweat equity as putting in the work to renovate and upgrade units, evict non-paying tenants, invest in the overall curb appeal of the building, and re-rent the units to higher-paying tenants at market rent.

When you go out of state, there are real opportunities to find a building and turn it around without so many governmental regulations, giving you the opportunity for faster and easier appreciation. This allows the investor to refinance their money out of the building faster or flip the property to an investor looking for a turn-key, no headache property to own and manage.

In 2018, I purchased an eight-unit apartment building in Phoenix with two other partners for $775,000. Rents were low, the units needed remodeling, and the exterior was in desperate need of a facelift. Existing rents were around $700-$725 for the two-bedroom units. My partners and I decided to raise the rent immediately because they were below market. Immediately, a couple of tenants moved out and we were able to remodel the units. Once remodeled, our management company was able to rent these two-bedroom units for $950-$975. We also decided to invest in giving the property a facelift. All in all, we spent a total of $45,000 on upgrading units and the building itself. We were able to sell the property less than one year later for $1,100,000. We achieved that price by raising the overall rents of the building to a higher number.

Business-Friendly Policies

Another advantage of buying out of state is working in business-friendly environments. The more conservative states have a more pro-business and pro-landlord philosophy. The average eviction process in Texas might take six weeks, while in California that same eviction could take six months. These more conservative states also have laws against or limiting rent control.

I worked with a couple who owned an 18-unit building in South Central Los Angeles. They were tired of dealing with the city's strict rental ordinances and other issues that came with owning in such a tough area. Through our analysis, we were able to show them that selling their property and purchasing out of state would significantly increase their cash flow more than selling and buying in a better part of Los Angeles. The couple was drawn to Arizona because of its land-lord-friendly laws and the ability to make significantly more money to help their family out. They settled on a 50-unit apartment building in Tucson, which increased their cash flow by 175 percent through a 1031 exchange.

What Should You Look For?

Some people ask me what they should look for in an investment property. I tell them that as a rule of thumb, if a property hits the market and it is significantly below the average per-unit price per square foot cost, then that is always something to take a look at.

When my team is looking for a multi-family property, we look for areas with dense population, good job growth, and vacancy rates that are low or trending lower. Lately, our Marcus & Millichap research department has been following a lot of growing tech companies and paying attention to where they are setting up shop. As multiple tech companies congregate in certain cities, they create significant job growth for millennials, who are one of the largest demographic of renters in the country. Portland, Oregon and Charlotte, North Carolina are great examples of this because of their growing tech sectors which have caused increases in population.

Paying attention to zoning laws is extremely important for investors as well. A city that has strict zoning laws is going to limit development. In Portland, barriers to entry for developers are high because of con-servation rights and the city's desire to be as environmentally friendly as possible. These regulations will slow new development and not allow for the oversaturation of new rental units. What this does is put a premium on the current stock of apartment buildings, as it causes rent to stay high with a significant lack of competition. Investing in an area with a ton of land and very loose zoning laws can become a nightmare for an investor. They might buy an apartment building and then right across the street, another investor might build a strip club or some other undesirable property could be built which ends up devaluing your investment.

Does a property have to be in need of updating? That question is always determined by a client's risk tolerance and what their goals are. A client looking for a more stable asset needs to concentrate on something that has proven itself through seasoned rents and overall performance. Stable assets can have both rental rates below market and closer to market. If rents are significantly below market value, you can almost assure yourself that the current landlord kept them low in order to also keep their ownership costs low. The less you charge a tenant, the less you increase a tenant's rent, the less likely they are to complain about small problems in the apartment building. There are a lot of landlords who have this mindset.

My advice to investors who are looking to purchase properties out of state, whether it is a turn-key property or a value-add property, you MUST hire a third-party management company to take care of it for you. You also, at the very minimum, need to visit the property once a month to check on it and to make sure the management company is doing their job. For properties that are value-add plays or need significant work, I would suggest the investor be out there two or three times a month. The advances in communication via Skype, email, smartphones, cameras, and more have allowed investors to remotely monitor their investments and keep track of progress. This allows them to be on top of what is going on. However, I cannot stress enough the importance of periodically making the trip to see the investment in person.

What Size Property Should You Invest In?

Multi-family properties are all about economies of scale. The bigger the property, the better the price. When our clients are looking to purchase out of state, we try to focus on properties that are 50 units or more. We believe that investors will have an easier path to higher income with more units. If you have a 100-unit apartment building and you raise the rent by $15 per unit, that equates to $1,500 per month and $18,000 per year. To increase rents by $18,000 per year for a 10-unit building, you would have to increase rents by $150 per month. The $150 per unit is much more difficult for that tenant to be able to withstand as opposed to a $15 per month increase.

When considering purchasing out of state, it is extremely important to travel to the property as well as spending a couple of days driving through the city or neighborhood to get a better idea of the neighborhood. Seeking advice from real estate professionals or local agents who can provide you with the necessary research, support, and information on changing regulations is crucial. Investors must seek some sort of professional guidance to make sure they are getting the best bang for their buck.

CHAPTER 13

ENHANCING YOUR BRAND AS A REAL ESTATE PROFESSIONAL

By **TENITA C. JOHNSON**

While many may think that a real estate professional should solely focus on the state of the economy, investment trends, and interior décor, every successful real estate professional also has a strong brand. Whether it's a memorable phone number, a catchy slogan, or a quirky jingle, it's now more important than ever to create consistent messaging for your target market.

People want to do business with those they know, like, and trust. The real estate industry is no different. If a real estate professional doesn't make their presence known early on in his or her career, he or she risks simply falling through the cracks of the large pool of professionals that already exists in an ever-changing, competitive market.

Erica found herself in that pool and couldn't dig her way out.

I met Erica through the Rochester Regional Chamber of Commerce in Rochester, Michigan. When we met, while she had a great reputation in and around Rochester for being a real estate professional, she was missing some of the key components required to take her brand to the next level. Fortunately, I was able to work with her to increase her brand awareness, expand her target market, and broaden her reach. We were able to do so by building her an engaging website, publishing a book that further positioned her as an expert in the industry, and using a ghostwriter to publish articles and blog content regularly.

Wow Your Customers With Your Website

Your website is your home away from home. It's the first place most people will visit once they've met you at a networking event or been referred to you by a friend. The challenge is once you get visitors there, you've got to keep them there. They must see something, hear something, or even feel something from the moment they enter your site to make them stay and click around a bit.

On the main homepage, site visitors need to know what you do, who you do it for, and why you do it like no one else. You can tell site visitors this in several ways. It can be an engaging short video that automatically plays as soon as they enter the site. It can be explained in a series of graphics that scroll at the top of the homepage, or your story can be told with a short one- or two-paragraph introduction. More importantly, within the first few moments a visitor is on your website, make sure your "ask" is clear and prominent. Maybe your goal is to get visitors to schedule a free consultation. Other times, it may be to get browsers to sign up for a free webinar you are hosting. You can even give them more value for free by integrating a pop-up box to gather email addresses by offering them a free electronic resource. These are called "calls to action," and their goal is to get the site visitors to interact with your website and take action. Even if visitors never click onto another page of the site, your main goal is to get some type of information to stay connected with them long-term.

In addition, every website should have some form of client testimonials. Again, this can be done through videos or short quotes from pleased clientele. It's great to toot your own horn, but it's even better when others do it for you. Ask every client for a 30-second video review, or a one- to two-sentence testimonial about their experience working with you and what set you apart from your competitors. Word-of-mouth and referrals are still the highest forms of compliment. Testimonials are a simple, yet profound way to increase your brand awareness and broaden your reach seamlessly. They also provide "social proof" of your expertise.

Besides a killer introduction and testimonials, you need an engaging professional bio. If your "About" page just reflects you as an individual, this page will hold only your bio and professional photo. Your bio should be no longer than 500 words. However, if you have a staff, also consider posting shorter bios of no more than 250 words each, coupled with each staff member's professional photo on this same page. This is a great place to introduce your entire team to site visitors.

More than educational accolades and industry achievements, your professional bio should highlight what sets you apart from the competition, what your passions are, and who you serve. Your bio should ultimately speak to the pain point or the problem of your target market—so they know that you are the solution.

Of course, you can have a contact page, market reports, industry trends, and area profiles. You may even want to add 360-view videos of homes and properties instead of the basic still photos for your listings. Whatever fits best for your brand, be consistent. Before you know it, your target market will be targeting you; you won't have to go find them.

Write a Bestselling Book

Breathe! You may be screaming inside your head, "I'm not a writer!" I get it. Not everyone is a writer, nor do they aspire to be a writer. However, I've got great news for you. You don't have to be a writer to author a book! You don't have to take a course. You don't have to be an English extraordinaire. You already have the secret sauce! You have the knowledge, wisdom, and passion for your specific industry. You know your clients' pain points and you have solutions to help them overcome those pain points. That equates to content. Don't overthink the process.

As simple as it may sound, an outline will be your best friend. It will keep you on track with your thoughts, and it serves as a guide for finishing your book in a timely manner. For example, if your book is about seven keys to real estate investment, your outline may be an introduction, one chapter to discuss each key, and a closing chapter. If your book is about how to stage a home for sale around the holidays, you could start with a short story of a family who desperately needed to sell their home before the holidays. And you could follow that with the five keys of staging homes to effectively sell, based on the five senses (sight, hearing, smell, taste, and touch).

You can easily self-publish your book, and once you have your book published in paperback form, consider converting it to an ebook and an audiobook. You can also use the key concepts in the book to develop a web course or workshop series to generate an additional stream of income. In addition, consider creating a shorter ebook (no more than ten pages) as a free download on your website, which highlights each concept, but with shorter teasers and explanations. Ultimately, once potential clients download the free resource, they'll be hungry to learn more and will buy the full book, which gives you another passive stream of income: book royalties.

Use what you have. You're already an expert in the industry, and your book will simply expand your reach and open greater doors of opportunity. Hire a professional cover designer, editor, typesetter/formatter, and publisher (or self-publish). Market and repeat!

If you don't consider yourself to be a great writer, or you simply don't have the time to get a book done and out quickly, consider hiring a ghostwriter. Most ghostwriters will work with you individually to gather your knowledge and expertise. This may consist of interviews, transcription of audio files or handwritten notes, or even dissecting videos of you speaking previously. The best part about using a ghostwriter is that you, as the author, get to maintain control over the process and the final outcome. A ghostwriter is paid one time to produce a product that you will reap residual benefits from.

Invest in a Blog Ghostwriter

Content is still king—in every industry. Again, people do business with those they know, like, and trust. If you're consistent about developing engaging blog posts, publishing articles in industry publications, and even pushing out quick tips on social media daily, you won't just be memorable. You will be at the top of their mind when potential clients need your services or products. If you don't consider yourself a writer, or you simply don't have time to kick out quality content that often, investing in a ghostwriter can take the responsibility off of you. Yet, you will reap all the benefits.

If you have the audio recordings from any speaking engagements, interviews, or panel discussions, your ghostwriter can transcribe the content and edit it so you can repurpose it for blog posts, social media graphics, or articles. These can be created from something as simple as a Facebook live or Zoom video, a blog talk radio interview, a podcast interview, or your latest interview with Fox News. Many real estate professionals become overwhelmed with the thought of producing new content and the amount of time it may take. That's the key. Learn to repurpose what you already have and present it in creative formats on various platforms.

You can also give a list of topics to your ghostwriter and have them create new blog articles in your voice, such as giving readers your top tips for working with mortgage lenders or the best negotiation tactics when submitting an offer on a new property. You can then post those blogs to your website and also have your ghostwriter repurpose them into social media quotes, video ideas, and more.

Reach out to industry publications and ask if you can publish an article in each issue. Most publications have both an online and print version for each issue, so that may yield exposure to two different audiences. Once you have a book, and you've had numerous speaking engagements and interviews, pulling content for articles is easy for a ghostwriter. People are watching (and reading) who you do not know. Your return on this investment is going to come when you least expect it.

The real estate marketplace sometimes feels like it is saturated with those who over-promise and under-deliver. Excellence and quality will always trump even the most qualified and well-versed real estate professional. When potential clients notice that you don't just work in the real estate industry, you've become all things real estate, they will naturally and organically be drawn toward you. Remember, your website, your book, and even your online articles need to speak to a potential client's pain points. The real estate world is full of people looking for solutions. You are that solution.

Remember Erica from the Chamber of Commerce? Today, her real estate business is doing much better than it was when we first met. She gets constant traffic to her engaging website and she has been featured in numerous industry-specific publications for her expertise and achievements. You don't have to be a website designer to create a killer website. You don't have to be a professional writer to author a book. And there's no shortage of ghostwriters! When you enhance your brand as a real estate professional, you won't just transform your own life; you'll transform the lives of those all around you!

CONCLUSION

By **ADAM TORRES**

As a publisher and podcast host, my audience comes to me for conflict-free advice that helps them along their path in life. This book serves as a culmination of differing opinions and expertise. The aim of bringing these authors together was to create a resource that would help people navigate the real estate market. Real estate is and will likely remain a major component of investment portfolios both in the United States and abroad. When evaluating your investment plan, it is important to get qualified individuals on your team. The following appendix lists the best route to contact the authors featured in this book.

To your success,

Adam Torres

P.S. Don't forget to listen to our podcasts at **MissionMatters.com**

APPENDIX

Adam Torres | Preface, Chapter 1 | Page iii, Page 1
Co-Founder Money Matters Top Tips
MoneyMattersTopTips.com
Instagram: @AskAdamTorres
Twitter: @AskAdamTorres

Benjamin Inman | Chapter 2 | Page 9
Managing Member, Inman Equities, LLC
InmanEquities.com
Phone: 615-513-3088
binman@inmanequities.com
LinkedIn: https://www.linkedin.com/company/inmanequities/
Facebook: https://www.facebook.com/inmanequities
Instagram: @inmanequities
Twitter: @inmanequities

Garrett Mott, Esq | Chapter 3 | Page 25
Shareholder, Hennigh Law Corporation
SAN FRANCISCO & LOS ANGELES
4 Embarcadero Center, Suite 1400
San Francisco, CA 94111-4164
(415) 325-5855
700 Flower Street, Suite 1000
Los Angeles, CA 90017
(213) 277-7226
Email: garrett.mott@hennighlaw.com

Harlan Gleeson | Chapter 4 | Page 33
Owner, Gallery Skan
www.galleryskan.com
harlan.gleeson@gmail.com
Instagram: @harglees

James Huang | Chapter 5 | Page 39

President, Sperry Commercial Global Affiliates

Principal and Founder, BRC Advisors

National President, Asian Real Estate Association of America

National Board of Directors, Asian Pacific Islander American Public Affairs

jhuang@brcadvisors.com

LinkedIn: https://www.linkedin.com/in/james-huang-3772839/

https://www.apapa.org/

Jeff Mount | Introduction, Chapter 6 | Page vii, Page 47

President, Real Intelligence LLC

jeff.mount@realintelligence360.com

Phone: (203) 529-4464

Linkedin: https://www.linkedin.com/in/jeff-mount-592596b/

Facebook: https://www.facebook.com/jeff.mount.3766

Twitter: @JeffMount5

Instagram: @Mount1760

Josh Whisler | Chapter 7 | Page 57

Founder of The Whisler Law Firm

www.whislerlawfirm.com

LinkedIn: https://www.linkedin.com/in/josh-whisler-08ba104

Business LinkedIn: https://www.linkedin.com/company/whisler-law-firm/

Facebook: https://www.facebook.com/TheWhislerLawFirm/

Twitter: @whislerlaw

Instagram: @whislerlaw

Mark Atalla | Chapter 8 | Page 69

Managing Partner and Founder of Carlyle Capital

https://www.carlylecapitalinc.com/

Instagram: @trademarkmark @carlylecapital

Facebook: https://www.facebook.com/CarlyleCapitalInc/

Personal LinkedIn: https://www.linkedin.com/in/mark-atalla

Business LinkedIn: https://www.linkedin.com/company/carlyle-capital

Ryan Cotter | Chapter 9 | Page 77

Market Leader at Movement Mortgage & Founder of the Real Estate Rumble

Facebook: @ryancotterloanofficer

LinkedIn: https://www.linkedin.com/in/ryan-cotter-b9a7519/

https://movement.com/lo/ryan-cotter

Real Estate Rumble

Facebook:@ReaEstateBoxing

www.Chicagorealestaterumble.com

S. Blake Harris, Esq. | Chapter 10 | Page 83

Managing Attorney, Mile High Estate Planning

1610 Wynkoop Street, Suite 550

Denver, CO 80202

Phone: 720-924-6171

www.MileHighEstatePlanning.com

Blake@MileHighEstatePlanning.com

Santiago Grossy, CAM, CMCA | Chapter 11 | Page 91

Regional Director, Affinity Management Services LLC

SMG@ManagedByAffinity.com

ManagedByAffinity.com

LinkedIn: http://linkedin.com/in/santiagogrossy

Business LinkedIn: https://www.linkedin.com/company/affinity-management-ser-vices-llc

Sevak Keshishian | Chapter 12 | Page 99

First Vice President, Marcus & Millichap

Sevak.Keshishian@MarcusMillichap.com

Phone: (818) 212-2694

LinkedIn: https://www.linkedin.com/in/theskgroup/

Facebook: https://www.facebook.com/skgroupcre/

Website: https://www.theskgroup.net/

Tenita C. Johnson | Chapter 13 | Page 107

CEO of So It Is Written

info@soitiswritten.net

Facebook: https://www.facebook.com/TenitaBestseller/

Twitter: @TenitaJEditor

Instagram: @mrstenita

On the web: SoItIsWritten.net

The Red Ink Conference

redinkconference@gmail.com

Facebook: https://www.facebook.com/redinkconference/

Instagram: @theredinkconference

On the web: TheRedInkConference.com

Listen to our
PODCASTS

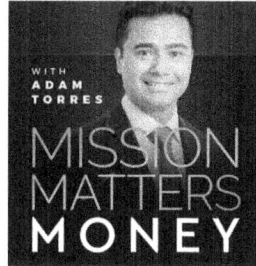

MISSION **MATTERS**
WE MAKE STORIES **BIGGER**

www.MissionMatters.com

The
PODCAST MATTERS
SCHOOL

Why Did I Start This School?

Every day, I interview business owners, entrepreneurs, and executives. I've done over 1,500 podcast episodes.

Depending on when you read this, I'll likely be over 2,000 episodes!

Many of the people I interview ask me to help them launch their own podcast. My ultimate goal is to help people spread their story and message. So, of course, I started helping people one by one. I figured that the more people I can help start podcasts, the more people I would help spread their message. Mission accomplished.

But then things got a little out of control. See, I have a habit of over-committing. It got to the point where helping people launch their own podcast was taking up more time than I had available.

So, I was faced with two choices.

One, I could tell people that I just don't have the time to help them.

Or, two, create a podcast school for those who want to launch a podcast or continue to grow their reach for an existing podcast.

I wanted to continue helping people, so the school was born.

What Makes This School Different?

First, this course is NOT designed for people looking for a way to make a quick buck.

The course is designed for busy professionals who have always wanted to start a podcast but have never had the time or knowledge to get one started. Others who will benefit from the teachings in this course are the part-time podcasters who can't quite figure out how to grow their audience.

While I'm not claiming that I've seen all podcast courses ever made, I can tell you that when I was first getting started, it seemed like all of the courses were really long and felt like part-time jobs just to complete. Well, I wasn't looking for a part-time job, I had a business already and I just wanted to podcast.

So, my commitment to you is that each lesson in this course will be straight to the point. Most videos are under five minutes and many of them are two minutes or less. Why? Because you don't need to hear me drone on. You just need the information so you can take action. Less time learning and more time in action is what will grow your podcast.

Finally, though it's kind of weird for me to say this considering I had almost 14 years of wealth management experience before going full-time into media about three years ago, but this is what I do for a living.

This is not a "side hustle" for me. I get paid to podcast, not just to teach. Why do I tell you this? Because you want to learn from someone who lives and breathes what they are teaching. You don't want someone experimenting with YOUR time.

For more information visit **MissionMatters.com**.

Happy Podcasting!

Adam Torrey

OTHER AVAILABLE TITLES

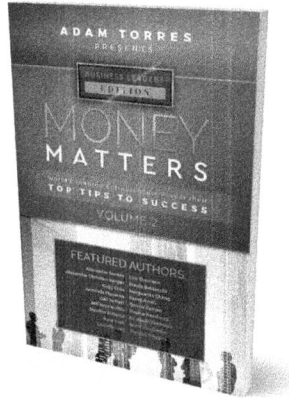

In the second edition of *Money Matters (Business Leaders Edition Vol 2)*, Adam Torres features 18 top professionals who share their lessons on leadership. In these pages, through inspiring stories, you'll discover:

- How to harness the entrepreneurial mindset.
- Why scaling your business for sustainable growth is vital.
- How to grow your eCommerce business.
- Lessons learned from sales experts.
- How to level up your leadership.
- How to manage your energy.
- And much more.

Purchase at **MissionMatters.com**.

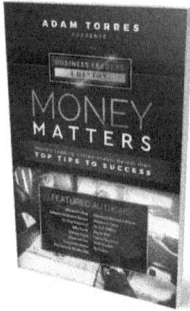

In the original edition of *Money Matters (Business Leaders Edition)*, Adam Torres features 15 top professionals who share their lessons on leadership. In these pages, through inspiring stories, you'll discover:

- How to create a clear path for growth.
- Why every business should act like a media company.
- How to build a community to last a lifetime.
- Lessons learned from professional soccer.
- How to maintain a well-connected brain for peak performance.
- How to create harmony through union in business.
- And much more.

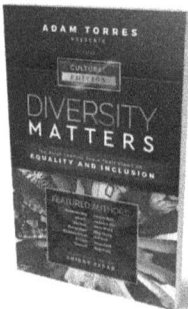

Embracing diversity and inclusion in a rapidly changing business landscape can be challenging. Are you and your organization positioned properly for this new age of connectivity? Torres features fourteen top Asian leaders who share their lessons on diversity, equality and inclusion.

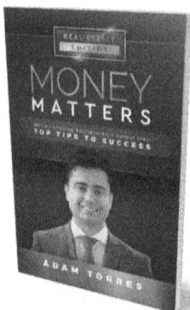

Navigating the world of real estate can be stressful. Are you getting closer or further from your goals? Finance guru Adam Torres is here to help you move forward. His guide, Money Matters, features 15 top professionals who share lessons from their more than 250 years of combined experience.

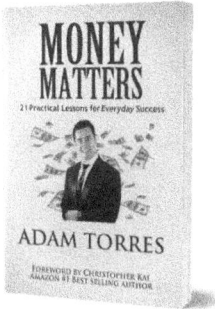

In this clear, concise manual, financial expert Adam Torres goes over the basics of personal finance and investing and shows you how to grow your wealth. Torres makes sure you are prepared for whatever life throws your way. It's never too early to think about the future and his book will give you the right tools to tackle it.

All books available for purchase at **MissionMatters.com**.

This workbook has been designed specifically for individuals like you who are dedicated to improving the results in all areas of your life. By following the ideas and exercises presented to you in this transformational workbook, you can move yourself into the realm of top achievers worldwide.

Download for free at **MissionMatters.com**